Catch the Spirit

Catch the Spirit

*Teen Volunteers Tell How
They Made a Difference*

Stories of Inspiration from 20 Remarkable Recipients
of The Prudential Spirit of Community Award

Susan K. Perry, Ph.D.

Franklin Watts
A Division of Grolier Publishing

*New York · London · Hong Kong · Sydney
Danbury, Connecticut*

To Stephen Perry and
All the unsung mothers of the world
who teach caring, compassion,
and community service
by example

Photographs ©: Courtesy of Alisia Orosco: 25; Courtesy of Anita Taylor: 69, 70; Courtesy of Ariane Wilson: 130, 132; Courtesy of Brian Harris: 60; Courtesy of Gabrielle Contreras: 37; Courtesy of Jamie Morales: 142; Courtesy of Jenny Hungerford: 78; Courtesy of Kristen Deaton: 94; Courtesy of Mark Lindquist: 43; Courtesy of Matt Nonnemacher: 148; Courtesy of Michael Harris III: 88; Courtesy of Molly Vandewater: 29; Courtesy of Stephen Perry: 191; Courtesy of Todd Wheeling: 136; Courtesy of Tyrell Nickens: 102; Courtesy of Yanick Dalhouse: 108; Mark Regan Photography: 23, 34, 74, 82, 90, 116; Parallax Productions, Inc.: 16, 50; Rocky Mountain News: 127 (George Kochaniec), 124 (Cyrus McCrimmon); Teen People: 146 (Britt Carpenter).

Perry, Susan K., 1946–
    Catch the spirit : teen volunteers tell how they made a difference / Susan K. Perry
      p. cm.
    Includes bibliographical references
    Summary: Individual teenagers relate their experiences in various types of volunteer activities.
    ISBN 0-531-11883-5 (lib. bdg.) ISBN 0-531-16499-3 (pbk.)
    1. Voluntarism—United States. 2. Teenage volunteers in social service—United States—Interviews.
[1. Voluntarism. 2. Teenage volunteers in social service.] I. Title.
    HN90. V64 P47 2000
    361.3'7'0973—dc21   00-027343

GROLIER
PUBLISHING

Table of Contents

Acknowledgments

Many thanks are owed to The Prudential Insurance Company of America; to Mark Friedman, who was the original editor for this project when he was with Grolier; to Lucia Raatma, the book's more-than-competent and oh-so-responsive editor; and to Linda Konner, who ably agented *Catch the Spirit* and persisted in getting it into print. My heartfelt appreciation goes to the young people who gave me such inspiring interviews, and to their parents who donated so much of themselves with so little recognition. My boundless gratitude, as always, goes to Stephen Perry, who makes life such fun.

Foreword

During the course of my career, I have been privileged to meet and work with many exceptional men and women. Yet, some of the most impressive people I have met over the past several years have been young people—like the ones in this book.

When Prudential launched The Prudential Spirit of Community Awards in 1995 to recognize outstanding school-age volunteers, we knew we would find some caring, energetic young people. But I am happy to say that our eyes were opened by the sheer number of youth volunteers we have found across the country, by the depth of passion and commitment they have demonstrated, and by the profound impact they have had on their communities.

Forget stereotypes. At a time when community involvement seems to be on the decline and media coverage of young people is focused on crime and excess, it is heartening to know that the stereotypes are wrong. Through The Prudential Spirit of Community Awards, we have found tens of thousands of youth volunteers who are acutely aware of the needs of others around them, absolutely determined to help in any way they can, and remarkably resourceful in tackling the challenges that stand in the way.

Their causes are as diverse as their backgrounds. They have been a source of aid and comfort to the sick, disabled, and disadvantaged. They have saved countless lives through health and safety initiatives, and through campaigns against drug abuse and violence.

They have built and restored community resources. And they have motivated and guided others to follow in their footsteps.

They are an inspiration to youth and adults.

Here are a few of their stories. Some will make you smile; some will make you cry. But all, I hope, will inspire others across the nation and around the world to "catch the spirit."

Art Ryan
Chairman and Chief Executive Officer
The Prudential Insurance Company of America
Newark, New Jersey

Introduction

It's always fun to read about others like yourself. If the young people you're reading about have taken on interesting challenges and succeeded, you may feel inspired to take action too. When you discover what makes them tick, what drives them, what gives them joy, you may be motivated also.

Catch the Spirit tells the personal stories of twenty otherwise perfectly typical teens who have given countless hours to start and run projects that help others. You'll learn about the variety of needs these teens discovered in their communities, from sick children who had no one to bring them a stuffed animal, to people who were going hungry, to youngsters who longed for "anything" for a holiday gift, to orphaned baby birds that needed care.

In each case, the teens took action after becoming aware of a need. Some of these volunteers were initially encouraged by a school program, a bar mitzvah requirement, a church, a parent, or a newspaper story, while others took action after seeing something that needed to be done in their neighborhood. They have each come to care deeply about those who don't have some of their own advantages.

Too good to be true? Not at all. These teens are not necessarily more altruistic, more unselfish, than those who gave less of themselves. They saw a need, felt strongly, and did something to make a difference. And once they started their projects, the emotional rewards began.

Get in Flow by Volunteering

It's possible, and actually quite likely, to feel really, truly good about yourself—to enjoy yourself—while doing good. Psychologists talk about a state of mind called "flow." You're in flow when you're so busy with some activity that you forget to worry about yourself and your surroundings. You might forget what time it is when you're in flow because what you're doing has become the most interesting thing in the world. It feels so good that you want to keep on doing it.

Many of the teens in this book have found that they can get in flow in their volunteer work. The community service they do makes them forget everything else while they're doing it, and they often wish there were more hours in the day so that they could pursue their projects even longer. Doing something because you want to, not because someone is grading you or paying you, is the best kind of motivation there is. It feels great!

Besides, having a goal is energizing, exciting. The busier you are—up to a point—the more you manage to get done. Also, the happier you are likely to be. One researcher studied several groups of young people in their mid-teens, and she found that teens who did volunteer work were happier than those who didn't. Happiness comes more readily to those who commit to something outside themselves. It gives a very powerful meaning to your life.

All the teens interviewed for this book shared, in simple words that can nevertheless give you chills, what has kept them going. It's always something like, "When I look into those kids' eyes, when I see their excitement, I can't describe how good it makes me feel. How can I not want to keep helping?" Such passion is always contagious.

Another way of looking at why these kids do what they do is to think about their strengths. They clearly have a kind of intelligence that exists beyond schoolwork, whether you call it emotional intelligence or interpersonal smarts. It's what makes these kids able to *feel* for others so intensely. It's one thing to feel, however, and another to act. Making a difference in the world starts close to home, and all the talk about great values doesn't mean much if you turn away from the need right in your own community.

We hope that these stories will show you how normal—and, also, how special—it is to be able to devote some time and energy to helping others.

The Truth about Teens and Volunteering

Teens do a lot of volunteering. A national telephone survey of 993 high school students was conducted in 1995 by the Wirthlin Group for The Prudential Insurance Company. It was found that 95 percent of teens believe it is important for people to volunteer their time to community activities. More than six out of ten teens say it's very important, that individual action is the best solution to community problems.

A study done in 1996 for Independent Sector by the Gallup Organization found that almost three out of five teens ages 12 to 17 volunteered in the past year, averaging 3.5 hours per week. More than one-third of all teens start volunteering by age 14.

One researcher found that there is no particular personality that all volunteering teens share. Rather, teens are more likely to volunteer if someone asks them, first of all, and then if a parent or an organization supports such service activities. In fact, most of the teens in this book give a huge amount of credit to their parents for encouraging and supporting them throughout their projects.

You will see in the following stories how all the teens empathize with those less fortunate. You may also notice, in many instances, their willingness to be different from their peers who didn't understand why they were devoting so much time to others. You'll also learn how they keep going when they face obstacles or fail to find as much help as they wanted. And you'll see what they have learned—about the world and themselves—from their challenging and enriching experiences.

The Prudential Spirit of Community Award

The twenty teens in *Catch the Spirit* were chosen out of the several hundred who have won state-level Prudential Spirit of Community Awards over the past five years. The award was created in 1995 by The Prudential Insurance Company of America in partnership with the National Association of Secondary School Principals, and it has been presented each year to one middle school student and one high school student in each state, the District of Columbia, and Puerto Rico. The awards program has recently expanded to Japan, Korea, and Taiwan.

Prudential's goal with this annual award initiative is to ignite the spirit of volunteerism in young people. Its purpose is to show that individuals of any age can have a significant impact on their own communities; to provide positive and realistic role models for both girls and boys; and to encourage young people to think about all the ways they can fulfill their own potential while putting their ideals into practice and doing good in the world.

In September of each year, application forms and instructions are sent to all United States middle-level and high schools, Girl Scout councils, and county 4-H organizations. From among the local honorees who are picked by those schools and organizations, state honorees are chosen. Ten of those state honorees are then named America's top youth volunteers of the year by a National Selection Committee of prominent figures at a ceremony in Washington, D.C., in May.

All Prudential Spirit of Community honorees are selected exclusively on the basis of their volunteer community service (unlike most other youth-recognition programs, which almost always take into account academic performance and other activities). The specific criteria used to judge the applicants are personal initiative, creativity, effort, impact, and personal growth. The state honorees are picked by a professional independent organization specializing in student evaluation. The national honorees are picked by a National

Selection Committee co-chaired by two United States senators and Prudential Chairman Art Ryan. This committee also includes the heads of several major youth and service organizations and other prominent individuals. For the past several years, the National Selection Committee has also included two national honorees from the previous year. (For contact information, see Appendix C.)

As exciting as it is to win a major award like Prudential's, none of the teens interviewed pursued their projects in hopes of winning something. The award always came as a nice surprise, a kind of extra bonus after all that work. And for most, it served another purpose: It helped get the word out about their projects.

"It's not just the award itself," says Ariane Wilson. "It's a really great trip to Washington, D.C., too. We had interesting activities in the hotel, got to see all the monuments, met the other winners, and got to exchange ideas. But what's even better is that a lot of people went home from hearing about my project thinking about doing something similar in their own communities."

In selecting those to represent all these terrific teens for this book, we sought for a mix of males and females, aiming for a variety of ages, backgrounds, geographical locations, and types of projects. In Appendix B, you'll find a batch of additional award-winners with their projects briefly described.

You will find that this is not so much a how-to book, though included is plenty of practical information that will make the task of volunteering easier. Instead this is more of a "why bother" book. You'll see why some young people bothered to make a difference, and surely you'll find these teens' enthusiasm for their projects inspiring. And being inspired is the first step toward acting on your own vision for a better world.

CHAPTER 1

David Levitt:

"People Have to Eat Every Day"

David Levitt, an almost 15-year-old from Seminole, Florida, looked forward excitedly to getting his driver's permit, exactly like most teens his age. Unlike most, though, David had already logged in numerous hours of contact with his local school board and government administrators, all in the hopes of getting food—that would otherwise be wasted—to those who need it. Still, even after the community-service project he started when he was only 12 turned out to be wonderfully successful, David believes he's really no different from any other kid. "I saw something I wanted, and I went for it." Because of David's tenacity, many hungry people are now eating regularly. And David has learned on a truly gut level that things get done in the world based on "how badly you want something."

David Levitt

The Sunday School at my temple always encouraged us to give money to the poor, but this project was the first time that I physically got involved with community service. It was mostly because my bar mitzvah was coming up, and you're supposed to do something good in the community. While I was considering what I ought to do, I read an article about Stan Curtis in *Parade* magazine. He had started all of the USA Harvest programs around the country. He had also come up with a partnership program with the Louisville, Kentucky, schools, called Operation Food for Thought. This is an all-volunteer transport network through which schools donate their leftover cafeteria food to be frozen and then delivered once a week to homeless shelters and so on.

That sounded like something I could do here in my own community. The first thing I did was volunteer myself (and my mom's driving) to Tampa Bay Harvest, because they were the ones who would be transporting the food from the schools to the homeless shelters or wherever.

My mother suggested that I talk to the principal of my school about getting Operation Food for Thought going here. When I asked him, he said it wasn't really his decision to make because there were federal guidelines or something like that. Back to my parents for advice. Luckily, my mother had worked with the school board before, and she suggested I contact them. First I wrote a letter to each school board member, including all the information they needed to know about the Harvest program. Then I followed that up with phone calls to see what each of them thought. They all loved the idea. My mother was able to get me on the agenda to speak at one of the school board meetings.

My turn to speak happened to be my birthday, the day I turned 12. After I spoke, the board members said, "Great idea, let's do it." But they would have to go through the health department and the people above them to be sure it was okay. They worked up a whole bunch of documents that would have to be signed.

Then they came back and said the health department was going to require we have plastic airtight containers for the food, and the school didn't have the budget for that. So I wrote letters to all the major manufacturers of plastic bags to get them to donate. I got a gift certificate from one store saying to come get whatever we needed, but other companies said they couldn't help since they get so many requests like mine. GladLock sent us a very short letter: "We appreciate your letter. Your shipment will be arriving in the next couple of days." They sent me eight humongous cases of plastic bags. And they continued to donate them on a regular basis whenever we needed them.

Finally, we were in business. That process took a whole year. Sure, I got kind of frustrated. I felt that the school board was just trying to put it off. I knew it shouldn't take a year just to get that much done. I noticed that each of the private companies wrote back within two weeks with a yes or a no. I certainly learned something about how bureaucracies work.

Fortunately, Stan Curtis had worked up a model for Operation Food for Thought that can basically be duplicated in any school system anywhere. So that was what we followed. It's not as if I had to invent something, but I had to struggle to get it implemented in my own school district.

At this point, I was in middle school, and kids were still into the teasing thing. They called me "charity boy," and even made some anti-Semitic cracks. It really didn't bother me that much. I guess they did that because I was doing something different and I was dealing a lot more with adults than I was with kids. All the teachers knew me, and the principal knew me by name the first week of school. And so the kids thought I was a little kiss-up or whatever. Or they were jealous of the attention I was getting.

Eventually, the school board approved the idea for the whole county, though it took a whole year before they let the schools start donating. Up to that point, all the extra lunch food got dumped right into the dumpster. The program started with a pilot project of 10 schools, one of which was mine. Then, during that year, more and more schools started donating. My mom coordinated volunteers for 20 of the schools, and 92 out of 155 schools in my district were participating. In one school year alone, 55,000 pounds [24,948 kilograms] of school food were donated to the hungry.

My main role now is as the inspirational person. I go around and do a lot of public speaking. Right now I'm working on getting the program expanded to the whole state. So I've been working with state representatives, talking to the food-service managers of the state.

My own awareness of the seriousness of the problem started from things I read in newspapers and magazines. But the real change came when my mom—she used to teach a senior studies course at our temple, which is for eleventh and twelfth graders—took me on a field trip to Everybody's Tabernacle, which is a homeless shelter in Clearwater. I learned a lot there. Basically all I know about what the shelters actually need and why people are there is from that visit. Seeing it in person hit me on a personal level. I learned that the homeless and hungry are turned away from shelters every day. When food is donated, money that is donated to these charities can be put to more long-term use, like teaching life and vocational skills.

I don't get teased anymore, at least not by my friends. In fact, they think what I'm doing is really cool. My friends thought it was a big thing just to be in the newspaper, and once I started getting awards, they said, "Ohmigosh, he's got another one." There's been so much publicity, which is really helpful. It just snowballs. Two of my friends go trick-or-treating with me every year for canned food. The mother of one of them volunteers with Tampa Bay Harvest. My old babysitter pledged time at a soup kitchen for a year after my bar mitzvah. So I've been able to have *some* personal impact on the people around me.

I learned that kids—any kid—can do anything. The world isn't based on seniority; it's based on how badly you want something. Although this was the first thing I've ever done on my own, I still had a lot of help. The weird thing is that adults had tried in the past to get that project going in our county, and I was told, "Don't get your hopes up. They've already shot it down a couple of times."

What keeps me going? Basically, it's because hunger and homelessness are such big problems. If everyone starts giving up when it gets hard, then nothing's ever going to get done. Maybe you'll get some food donated here or there, but nothing like a steady thing. Nothing will really change. The need for food is year-round, not just on holidays when people start donating. No person only eats during the holidays. They have to eat three times a day.

I don't really see myself as different from other kids in my school or anywhere. I saw something I wanted, and I went for it. I'm sure if one of my friends wanted an A in one of his classes, he'd study his butt off for it. If someone wanted to get a bike, he'd scrimp and save all he could. It's just something I wanted, and I went for it.

Besides my parents, my main role model would have to be Stan Curtis, who founded Harvest USA and Operation Food for Thought to feed the hungry. What impresses me about him is that he's a stockbroker, a vice president of his company, a big businessman, but on top of that, he has a heart, and he knows what people need, and he does his best to get it for them.

Through all these contacts with top-level administrators, I've learned to be myself when I call people to try to get something from them. I find that when a kid comes up and addresses adults, it's a nice change of pace instead of all these adults coming up and complaining. That's really the best part of all this. I discovered you don't have to be an adult to get something done. Everyone's always saying, "You're too young for that." But kids can actually do good things.

CHAPTER 2

Alisia Orosco:

Every Child Needs a Hug

Whenever Alisia Orosco and her family would visit her very ill baby brother in the hospital, they'd bring him his Pooh bear or another favorite stuffed animal. After dozens of these visits, when Alisia was 9 years old, she couldn't help but notice that many other little kids were getting neither loving visits nor gifts. She decided to change that, and began Every Child Needs a Hug. With allowance money and help from others, Alisia distributed hundreds of stuffed animals to hospitalized children throughout Texas. Even after her brother died and her mother became seriously ill, Alisia continued the project— "to honor them," she explains.

My baby brother David had to be in the hospital more than fifty times because he was born hydrocephalic with a seizure disorder. When we were visiting him during the time he had his first brain surgery, I saw that there were little boys in the beds on each side of him. No one was visiting them, so I asked about them and was told they'd been abandoned. It seems they had been left there by their parents because they were too sick and the parents weren't able to care for them. One had cerebral palsy like my other brother Georgie, and the other had tubes that fed him. I was amazed to find out that the hospital legally *owned* them. I also realized that they were very sad. And that made me cry.

Whenever we visited David, we would always bring him one of his stuffed animals from home to comfort him, and that would make him happy. So I asked my mom if we could bring these other little boys something too. At the time, we didn't have the money, so she said maybe next time.

Then it struck me that every time we went to the hospital there were some kids who were really unhappy, who didn't have anybody there for them very often. I was told that some of them were there because of abuse at home. I decided I wanted to do something about that.

The year David turned 3, I wanted to do something special for him. We bought him a new stuffed animal. I also put my allowance and my brother Georgie's allowance together (he's a couple years younger than me) so we could buy some stuffed animals for the other kids in the hospital for Make a Difference Day. It's a day when volunteers all over the country do projects to help their communities.

After Georgie and I put our allowances together, my mom added in a few dollars too, and then we went out and bought fifteen stuffed animals. I always used to tell my little brother he was special, and I wanted the other kids to feel like somebody felt that way about them too. I cut out paper hearts and wrote on them,

Alisia Orosco

"You're somebody special," and on the back I put my address. I tied these hearts around the neck or the arm of the stuffed animals. We sent them to the University Medical Center because they're the ones who helped my brother with that first surgery.

The nurses gave the animals out to the kids. David was in critical condition at that time so we couldn't do it ourselves. He was at home, and the doctors said he was probably going to die soon. Then he died of respiratory failure the next month.

Some of the parents of the kids who got that first batch of stuffed animals sent me letters thanking me. I knew I wanted to keep doing this because of the letters I had gotten that said the gifts made the children happy. Now I do it every year on Make a Difference Day, and sometimes I've given animals to children I've read about who were hurt in accidents. About a month after each Make a Difference Day, I start getting stuff together again for the next one.

The second year I got 235 animals for about $5 each and sent them out to different places. Over the months of that year my mom and I had put some on layaway. Two of my best friends helped me put the hearts on. The third year we had a little pizza party, and twelve kids helped me out. Some of them also contributed money. Some of them also helped us deliver the stuffed animals to places like Big Brothers/Big Sisters, Youth Guild, Hospice Rainbows Program (for kids who have lost a loved one), Noah Project (for kids from abusive situations), University Medical Center, and other places.

I gave $1000 worth of toys this year to Big Brothers/Big Sisters. We did a bake sale that made about $400, and Wal-Mart gave us a matching grant, which paid for a TV and videos we gave to a charity. We also gave art supplies to the Youth Guild for handicapped kids where Georgie goes.

Now, as people around the city have heard about what we're doing, a lot of them are giving me donations. The manager where my dad works donated a bunch of toys. We are planning a garage

Alisia Orosco and her stuffed animals brought hope to dozens of sick children.

sale to help out too. I've written lots of letters to companies, giving them information about my project and asking them for stuffed animals, school supplies, or arts and crafts. I told them they could send the toys in memory of, or in honor of, someone they love.

The first year all I got was letters and a couple of pictures of the kids enjoying the gifts, and I said, "You know, I wish I could be there." The second year we drove up to Lubbock and got to see some of the kids. We cried. It was really emotional, especially since it was the first time we'd been up there since my brother's death. My friends cried too, seeing all those children in the hospital. This fourth year we did get to go to the hospital here in Abilene and hand out the stuffed animals ourselves. You get to see their reaction, which makes all the effort really worthwhile.

When I told my friends about what I was doing the first year, they weren't sure about it and didn't really understand. Once I won the award, a lot of people wanted to help me, but some of them weren't really serious about it. This year, it was basically the same friends who have stuck with me. The girls who were with me the second year are still helping.

It was harder than I expected. At first, I just thought, "Oh, I'll get a few stuffed animals and send them." But then more people wanted to help, and people were writing to me, and I'd have to respond to them. People from all over the neighborhood wrote me and my friends from school. They would say, "You're doing a good job." If they just say congratulations, I won't answer any more, but if they donate something, then I write to thank them. Besides all that, I'm shy, and I had to learn to reach out and meet new people. I discovered that if you write to companies, they will help a lot of the time.

It's also really hard for me to go into hospital rooms and see the sick kids because it reminds me of David, and I miss him so much.

My advice to other kids who are thinking of helping others is that if you believe you can do it, then you can, if you stick to it. If you think you can, but you just quit, then it's not going to happen. The only difference between me and those kids who didn't want to bother helping after all is that helping makes me feel good. The best part has been knowing that I'm making other people feel good. Maybe they smile and actually know somebody cares about them.

CHAPTER 3

Molly Vandewater:

The Eyes of a Hummingbird

Molly Vandewater, who was a student at La Reina High School in Thousand Oaks, California, when we spoke, spent nearly every spare minute tending orphaned and injured animals. None of her friends understood why she gave so much time to this form of community service, but all you have to do is listen to Molly talk about how the animals make her feel, and you get it. Though cleaning cages and feeding baby birds is hard work, it's anything but a chore; rather, it's the most truly meaningful effort in her life.

I've always had pets, but caring for needy animals wasn't my idea in the first place. In fact, it all started accidentally with my dog. When I was in seventh and eighth grade, my family and I were living in Tucson, Arizona, way out in the country. One day my dog dug up a nest in a pile of sand and found some baby cottontail rabbits. The dog caught and killed two of the baby rabbits before we could stop him, but then we took in the remaining four. My mom and I went to the pet store and bought some kitten formula, and we just did what we thought was best for the animals. I raised them, and they survived.

After I had the baby rabbits for about a month, we found out about Lewis and Janet Miller of Wildlife Rehabilitators in Tucson. I turned the rabbits over to them. I got to go on the release—putting the animals back into the wild—which was an amazing experience. Every time I'm involved in releasing an animal, giving it a second chance, I get a thrill that's hard to put into words.

The Millers asked me to volunteer with them because cottontails are one of the hardest animals to rehab, and I had done so well with those four. So of course I wanted to. I went once a week and cleaned cages. As time went on, I got more and more involved. Then after about a year and a half, my dad got transferred back to California, where we had lived before. I wanted to stay involved in wildlife rehab but there was no one right in Thousand Oaks, where I live, doing rehab. So I joined a bunch of rehabbers who were just then trying to form a group. It's now called Wildlife Care of Ventura County.

We turned our extra bedroom into our little bird room. Though my parents like animals, they were mainly being supportive of me. It was really my thing. But as I got more involved, they got more involved too. Of course, since I was young, my mom had to drive me to meetings and such. Now we both do rehab together, because she has to take over my tasks while I'm at school.

Molly Vandewater

The busiest time is from April through August, though animals with injuries are brought in all year round. Bird injuries are caused by anything from cars to cats, or they fly into windows. When anyone in the public finds an injured animal, they call their vet or Animal Control. Since most of these agencies in our area have our number, they usually treat and release the animals to us for rehab. A local vet clinic, Conejo Valley Veterinarians, has been particularly helpful in providing treatment for free to the injured animals that come to us. If you don't have a license, it's illegal to keep any animal more than forty-eight hours, and our group has a special license.

That first season, all I got to rehab was two baby birds. Now we have three squirrels. One was hit by a car. We also have a mother possum and her six babies. She had been attacked by a dog and wasn't eating or feeding her babies, so I had to hand-feed all of them, but now they're all eating on their own. We also have an adult male possum that was dog-attacked, and we just got in a pelican. We get a lot of pelicans that either can't find food or got hit by a car. We only care for them for a couple of days if we need to, because we don't have a pond to house them, and then we send them on to Santa Barbara for care. We also have lots of different birds. The birds always outnumber the mammals.

Wildlife Care is still growing. Since the beginning we've taken in over 1,000 animals. One person in our group writes plans for us. Another transports animals. At our house, we do most of the animal rehab. We can have up to 150 wild animals at any one time, though right now we have probably about forty, including all the birds.

I did the intake forms too, which we turned in to the California Department of Fish and Game, which licensed us. The paperwork is my least favorite part. I hate forms!

I don't really have any favorite animals. Ask anyone who knows me: I love them all. But it's a lot of work to keep everything from smelling. The whole family helps clean cages. Whatever needs to be done gets done. It's not that hard: You just look in the cage and you can tell who needs to be fed or which cages need to be cleaned. I've taught my younger brother to feed baby birds so he can do it when I'm at a wildlife meeting.

Baby songbirds get fed every hour. The most time-consuming job of all is taking care of the baby hummingbirds. They get fed every fifteen minutes from 7:00 in the morning until 10:00 at night. We use the outside plastic sheath from a catheter, which is about the size of a needle, to feed them, with a syringe. If my mom has to take me to the orthodontist, for example, we pack them up in special little white drums like little incubator boxes, and we put little heat packs in the boxes, and we just bring them with us. Baby hummingbirds can start coming in as early as January and as late as late August. This past season we cared for about sixty-five baby hummingbirds. It's a *lot* of work. Sometimes when we get newborns in, with the shell still on them—we call them peas with heads.

What makes me do it? When I walk out into our bird room, and all these baby birds spring up and open their mouths for food, I just get really excited to be able to be a part of their lives and to be able to help them. I'd feel guilty if I said no to animals. I feel responsible. But also, I just like doing it. When I walk into there, I get this feeling. . . . I get so excited that I sometimes can't even catch my breath. I think birds are incredible animals. Well, I think *animals* are incredible. Some of the things animals do, the way they manage to survive, it gives me a great respect for all of them.

It's surprising how much people don't know about wildlife. We get people who call and say, "We've got squirrels in our backyard. How can we get rid of them?" Or "How can we kill them?" It's upsetting. One woman moved way out into the country and called and said, "There are coyotes. How can I get rid of them? Will you come trap them?" I told her, "No, they're in their home." We get a lot of phone calls like that. We're trying to do some educational programs to educate more people about living with wildlife.

Right now, I'm pretty sure I want to be a vet. I've been to meetings all across the United States, and I've collected lots of books and information about animals. I took biology last year and in the summer I started volunteering at Pet Emergency, so I could apply what I learned at school there.

Unfortunately, my friends aren't really into animals. I brought two of my friends home once, and they saw the baby birds and they really thought I was crazy. It's not that I don't have friends. I do, and sometimes I tell them about my animals because I get excited. But it's uninteresting to them. One day we were sitting at a lunch table outside and I saw a goldfinch, and I was totally interested. And they laughed. Whenever I see a bird in the trees, I look up and want to know what it is. I can tell what they are by hearing their voices. And my friends think it's kind of funny.

Most people think it's really gross to clean incubators that are full of poop. You just get used to it because it's what the bird needs. We have volunteers come sometimes, and people who bring birds to us sometimes say, "Oh, I'd really like to come and help." So we work with them, and some of them work really hard. But most of the time they don't stay when they find out how much work it really is. Birds are messy, and people really don't like the mess.

I think what it takes is a really strong love for animals. I've never been a really neat, clean person myself, but because I love the animals I'll go out and clean them and do whatever they need.

One of the hardest parts of this kind of work is trying not to get too attached to the animals. The season I raised my first two baby raccoons, and I knew I had to release them within the following two weeks, wasn't that easy for me. We're not supposed to name them, because then you'd get attached. And then once you name an animal, you're kind of taming it, because it learns its name. And it's not good for them to be tamed. That's why we have pets, so we can play with them and cuddle them. Then you don't have to go out and handle the wildlife.

Taking care of wildlife is a *job*. You do it for the animals so that they can go back into the wild. Some people want to volunteer to cuddle the animals. They don't realize you don't get to cuddle or play with the baby animals. We especially don't have *time* to do that. I get up at 5:00 in the morning and do my homework. During baby bird season I have no idea how I get my work done. I start feeding them at 7:00, then go to school, and when I get home I take over feeding them again. We try to at least put all the baby birds to sleep by 10:00, but sometimes we've stayed up past midnight feeding baby squirrels or just making sure everything is done, such as cleaning injured animals.

One of the lessons I've learned from all this is that sometimes people don't do what they say they'll do. Since I've been involved with this group, I've worked with some adults who act very childishly. Sometimes people work with the animals just so they can tell people they do it, to make themselves look better. I've learned as much about human nature as about animal nature.

When I think about myself and how I was back in sixth grade, I'm really not the same person. I have so much more confidence now. When you do a community service, you're doing something to help another living creature, and that makes you feel good about yourself.

Sometimes I do get sick of all the work. When that happens, I grab one of my bird books and go in my room and just look at the pictures of the birds. Just seeing them in the wild calms me down. Or sometimes I'll just go sit in the bird room anyway. I won't be doing anything, I'll just be watching the baby birds. When I look into their eyes, they just make me melt. I can't get mad at them.

Gabriella Contreras

CHAPTER 4

Gabriella Contreras:

Club B.A.D.D.D. Does Good

It's both frightening and frustrating to watch gangs and drugs on the loose in your neighborhood. When Gabriella Contreras of Tucson, Arizona, was just a third-grader, she and her friends found themselves observing the gang-related happenings at the high school across the street. They wished there were a way to make them stop. Luckily, Gabriella didn't just wish—she started Club B.A.D.D.D. From going on peace marches around the school to participating in a variety of fund-raisers, the club founded by Gabriella has made a real difference in the community. Along the way, she has learned how to tap into resources and work with others to cause change—instead of just looking across the street and feeling helpless.

I found myself volunteering really early. When I was about 5 years old, my mom was running an elder-care home. Whenever she would have activities there at the home, I volunteered to help out. Also when I was 5, I remember watching TV, and there was a commercial asking for help at the community food bank here in Tucson. "Just go ahead and call," the show said, and I asked my mom if I could. She said okay, so long as we made sure I wasn't too young. The food bank people were surprised when I called, since I was so young!

When I was in the third grade and 9 years old, there was a high school across the street from my school. Me and most of my friends were getting more and more worried because the high school was having a lot of riots due to drugs and gangs. The SWAT team came and blocked off the streets, which scared us. We could see right through the gate, right across the street, that there were a lot of not-so-great things happening there. My friends were wishing somebody would do something, and I said, "Hey, we can be the people who do something. Let's start something."

I think this attitude comes from my mother raising me to be the person who always does something, never saying "let someone else do it." I feel that's very important, because otherwise nothing gets done.

When my friends and I first started marching against violence during lunch, we would simply march around with posters. The posters, made from used construction paper collected from teachers, said, "Give hugs, not drugs" and "Stop the violence." Just a handful of my friends were involved then, and even my mom didn't know about it. Then during the summer I told her about it, and that I wanted to start a club. She said it sounded like a great idea, and that I should talk to my principal, Dr. Conrado Gomez. When I began fourth grade, I asked him if I could start an official club about making a positive difference. He said he would help out however he could.

Gabriella Contreras organized many student marches for
Club B.A.D.D.D.

The club I founded for kindergarten through eighth grade is called Club B.A.D.D.D., which stands for "Be Alert, Don't Do Drugs." Our motto is "Even as youths, we can make a positive difference in our home, in our neighborhood, in our school, and in our community." We always say that at the beginning of our meetings.

We had planned to use the principal's office to meet, but at that first meeting, there were too many kids who wanted to join. So we met at the library, but we always had to stay quiet there. I asked my fourth-grade teacher Dale Lopez if we could use his room at lunchtime instead, which is what we've been doing since then, once a week on Mondays. It's our sixth year now. A lot of the same people are still coming, and lots of new ones keep joining.

The club does a lot of different things. Once a week we cut out newspaper articles that discuss youth issues, and that motivates us. We decide which things to help with. A major one is the annual peace march for our school. It's an opportunity for the whole school to get involved, including the teachers, the students, and their parents if they want to. Usually over 500 people are there, and the media has covered it.

We have holiday parties and food drives for our school, when we go door-to-door collecting cans and such. And we also involve other students from our school by having contests to see who can bring in the most cans. We have gift drives for Christmas, and we make Valentine's Day cards. We sponsor events for our whole school too, such as "Entertainment Under the Stars," with folklorico and mariachi orchestras and bands performing. Both adults and young people join in, and neighbors and different neighborhood associations are invited too.

After being an Arizona Youth Delegate for America's Promise at a National Presidential Summit in Philadelphia, I became motivated to organize our own community-wide City Youth Summit, which Club B.A.D.D.D. helps sponsor. When I was in the sixth grade, we had over forty different booths, which involved many local organizations that use volunteers, whether youth or their parents. It was an awesome event with more than 500 people attending. All these young people were going around to these booths picking up brochures and stuff, as though they were trick-or-treating, and they were having a great time while they were learning about how to get involved.

Another regular event is our anti-violence, anti-drug art gallery. This is where we have Club B.A.D.D.D. members draw pictures of what they would like to see in a world without violence or drugs. Those pictures are then displayed in the library, and the whole school attends. Other clubs are invited to contribute art too.

We have learned how to ask guest speakers to come talk to us about drugs and violence and other subjects that relate to serving the community. We've been involved in the Nurses' Eyeglasses Fund, the Library Fund, March of Dimes fund-raising, and a Baby Heart Fund that raised $250 for a baby's operation. We raised $350 for students to attend a science field trip.

When this club had barely started, I remember there was a lot of vandalism in the bathrooms and the hallways, and we used to get graffiti on the school walls. And now, they don't do it as much. It still happens, and once in a while there's a fight, but nothing like what it used to be.

It wasn't hard to motivate a lot of kids to join Club B.A.D.D.D. because the way we hold the meetings, they think it's fun. Everyone's friends are there too. We all take turns opening and closing the meetings, and basically, I'm not the one who's running it. Everyone runs the meetings. We just write down the agenda, vote on it, and then start. We read our motto at every meeting, and we vote on the projects we're going to get involved in.

My mom and dad are not only very supportive, but they're the club supervisors. That way we have adults to be sure that everything's okay. They take turns, because they're divorced.

As busy as I am with club activities, I also have time to hang out with my friends. I go to concerts and parties and the mall. I'm an A-B student. I set my priorities. I first study, and after my homework is done, I either have fun or get involved, which is fun too. I'm on many community youth boards, as well as the National 4-H Youth Board. I meet more people that way, and by getting involved, I make more friends. I am a teen, so at times, I do push my homework aside, but most of the time I put it first.

I plan on going to college, and I want to study abroad for at least a year. I was in Berlin this summer at a Youth Summit celebrating the coming down of the Berlin Wall. I learned so much from that.

We applied for and won a $2,500 grant to create a packet to spread Club B.A.D.D.D. across the nation. This year I've been going around to different elementary schools and showing them the packet and video. My mother's friend helped us out with the video-taping. In the summer, I'm planning on responding to all those young people who've been writing me from different states about how to start clubs in their own schools.

The reward of getting involved, really, is knowing that you're making a positive difference. When we give the Valentine's Day cards that we've made to the elderly at the care facility, we see their smiles. To tell you the truth, yes, there are certain students in my school that make fun of me or of other students who join the club. I feel that if they could only spend at least one day in our club or just one day getting involved, they would really change their whole perspective.

CHAPTER 5

Mark Joon Park Lindquist:

An Opportunity to Give Back

Mark Joon Park Lindquist's features and his Korean middle name are the only clues to his birth outside Ortonville, Minnesota. Adopted at the age of eight months, Mark loves small-town life where you know everyone and there is really no such thing as a stranger. He says no one in Ortonville ever made him feel different, "which I think makes me very lucky." Seemingly a natural leader, Mark went from being involved in simple charity suppers to gathering the support of a large number of his schoolmates when another town was struck by a devastating series of tornadoes. Inspired by the way his own town was helped by others after a major flood the year before, Mark relished the chance to give something back. In a matter of a very few days, he rounded up an *astonishing $1,500, disaster supplies, and a busload of volunteers to help folks they'd never met before.*

Rather than focusing on his own role of initiating the project, Mark seems to take genuine delight in how he brought the joys of service to his friends and neighbors. One of his favorite memories is the way people who had never before experienced the feeling of helping others got to do so: "It was fun to see that surge of sudden energy."

My dad was in the Peace Corps, way back when, and it's possible that subconsciously that was an inspiration for me to get involved in community service. I know he instilled a lot of the values that make me the type of person I am. While my parents always encouraged me to be active, they never forced me, and in fact, sometimes they'd say, "Gee, Mark, are you getting in over your head?" A lot of times, I'd bite off a lot, but I was always the type of person who said, "Nope, I'm going to aim high, and I'm going to achieve my goal."

A Key Club International branch was started in my high school when I was an eighth-grader. Key Club (the youth branch of Kiwanis) is the largest high school service organization in the world. It's open to ninth- to twelfth-graders, and I was pretty heavily involved with it throughout high school. We do all sorts of different projects around our school and our churches and in our community.

Let me give you an idea of the size of my town: Ortonville has only 2,000 people. Our high school is seventh through twelfth grades, and even the kindergarten through sixth grades are all in the same building. My graduating class was about seventy people. We had about fifty members in the Key Club, spread out over four grades.

Mark Joon
Park Lindquist

I think community service thrives in a small town because you know everybody. Everyone helps everyone else and doesn't even think about it. It's just a given that people will lend a helping hand when it's needed.

I really started getting into community service when I was a sophomore. I guess it's true that sometimes we'd struggle to find something to do. Now I'm helping out with the Key Club at the high school here in Moorhead, where I go to college and there's 30,000 people, and there's never a shortage of things to do. But back home we'd wash fire trucks, clean ditches along the sides of the highway, paint the playground. We'd put on spaghetti feeds and pancake breakfasts and benefit suppers and raise money for people. The usual small-town stuff.

Still, I was drawn to community service, even that everyday unexciting kind, because there's just something special about Key Club that all the other school clubs don't have. When I got into Key Club, the motivation was not "What can you give me?" "What can I win?" or anything like that. It's all about helping others. There's a certain spirit, there's just something about giving yourself to others and not ever looking for any recognition or reward. Because of the people I'd meet and the things the organization stood for, the values and the goals, I was hooked. At first, I didn't even know what it was, I just knew, "I've got to stick with this." Eventually I realized it was just that giving of yourself to others makes you feel good.

The tornado project, which I won the Prudential award for, only lasted a week, but it had its start, its inspiration, about a year and a half earlier. I'll explain. We had a huge winter the year I was a sophomore. Sure, Minnesota has serious winters, to say the least. But this one was amazing, one of the largest snowfalls the state has ever had. I think we missed fourteen days of school because of snow, and it's got to be pretty bad for them to call a snow day.

The following spring, since there was so much moisture from the snow, we had quite a big flood. The ground was saturated, and all of Minnesota was under water. The town of Ortonville is on Big Stone Lake, one of the largest lakes in Minnesota, and we have the Minnesota River also. So our town was especially susceptible to this flood.

We were let out of school, and the community just dropped everything and pitched in to help strangers—though of course everyone really knew each other. The amazing thing to me was that people from all over the state, from hours and hours away, either packed up a bus full of supplies or filled up a bus with people and came down and helped sandbag. They were helping absolute strangers.

That provided a lot of the motivation and drive for my own project. The next spring, a tornado swept through St. Peter, Minnesota, a town of 10,000 people, which is five hours away from my town. We were still sort of cleaning up from our own flood of the year before, so it was still very clear in our minds what it was like to go through something like that.

On a Sunday, I heard on the news that a tornado had swept right through the middle of St. Peter. They were calling for volunteers and supplies, so I wrote down the number. The Salvation Army and the Red Cross were setting up emergency sites.

I realized this was our opportunity to give back. It just made sense. On Monday, I made some phone calls around the town and got the ball rolling. I called the Salvation Army and Red Cross to find out what was needed. On Tuesday, I called a meeting in the high school and put some announcements on the radio and in the newspaper. My plan was to take a busload of people and supplies to St. Peter on Saturday. When I asked people to help out, or made a call to someone asking for their time or donations, there wasn't even a second thought from anybody in the community. It was almost like my job was too easy. Without anybody having to tell them, people realized, "Hey, this is what we have to do."

There were a lot of details to arrange in a short time. I found a bus driver, arranged for chaperones, I got churches to be drop-off sites for donations of supplies, which we then had to collect on Saturday. I got help with all this by putting announcements on our local radio station and at the high school, held informational meetings, and contacted teachers and parents for help.

Once the ball got rolling, we just took off, collecting supplies, picking things up from different communities. A lot of people had been displaced from their houses and needed basics—toiletries, toothbrush, towels, canned food, stuff like that. Even the small surrounding communities from a few miles away pitched in. Kids from the high school would sit down at the grocery store with a little table and a sign saying "St. Peter Disaster Relief," and everybody that walked by would pitch in somehow, or as they went through the store they would buy some supplies and donate them when they got done, or they'd come back after they went home and give something. The school was totally cooperative, because they knew it wasn't just a bunch of kids skipping school.

On Saturday, we left real early with fifty-two volunteers, forty-nine of them from the high school, which to me is amazing. I've been involved in projects before and never had a turnout like that. Remember how small my school is. People who had never been to a Key Club meeting or involved in anything like that in their lives, they saw the need too.

At the beginning of that week, I had thought, "Let's raise $500 and let's get about twenty-five people to help." I figured that was shooting a little high for fund-raisers around that school. But in a matter of three days we raised $1,500 and had fifty-two volunteers. That goes down in history as our all-time high.

When we arrived at St. Peter, we checked in at the disaster sites and found where they needed help. Anything and everything, we did it. We spent a long time at a junkyard where all the junk had been blown around, mostly sheet metal, and for two hours we picked insulation off twigs and grass in a field because the birds would have been harmed by that.

We went out to a farmhouse and burned twigs and trees that had fallen down. I remember hearing the mother of the family commenting, "How neat it is to see a bunch of school kids give up their Saturday to come down and help total strangers." But in a way, it didn't feel like total strangers. Because they're living the same kind of life as us, and it could happen to any one of us. We'd learned that from our flood.

I didn't know what to expect when I was riding the bus on the way down there. When you see it on the news on TV and on the front page, you just hear about these things and you just keep moving. But just to see the devastation that has struck, it really made you almost smile in a way inside, because you knew that this is why we were here, because they need us.

Now I'm an elementary-education major in college. I think that being a teacher is the only thing I'll ever do. And definitely in a small town somewhere. I want to make a difference in people's lives. I'm also an advisor for the Key Club at the local high school here. I plan to do that forever. It's really been a part of me.

A lot of aspects of the tornado project will always stick with me. There's one from the week before the project, even though those days are almost like a blur to me—it all happened so quickly. Other times, working with other projects, say painting the playground, I'd ask for volunteers and it was like pulling teeth. But when I mentioned this project, people jumped at it. It was something special to see.

When people mention the term "community service," it's not always looked at in a favorable light. Some people tend to think, "Well, gosh, we gotta go do this work." But when you make it fun, it can be a heck of an experience. So when we were in St. Peter, we were tactful and respectful of the families and things like that, but the kids were having fun doing the service. That was fun to see. It wasn't like you had to twist someone's arm to carry that piece of sheet metal to the pile. They wanted to. They felt really useful.

After the project was over and done, when I'd be at school or around town, people didn't say, "Hey, we did this," and let everyone know. It was just something that they knew had to be done, and they didn't think anything of it. They weren't looking for the pat on the back. That was neat.

CHAPTER 6

Emily Douglas:

Grandma's Gifts

Emily Douglas's family originally came from Appalachian Ohio, an area with many people living "in challenging conditions," as Emily phrases it. After her beloved grandmother died, Emily found a way to honor the memory of her grandmother's generosity by starting Grandma's Gifts. She solicited contributions from Columbus, Ohio, inhabitants who had come from the Tri-State area (Lawrence County, Ohio; Boyd County, Kentucky; and Cabell County, West Virginia). With these donations, Emily purchases toys, clothes, and educational items for needy children in the Appalachian area.

What's most amazing about Emily's community service is how intense she is about it. In spite of the resistance of most of her friends, in spite of the tears

Emily Douglas

and frustrations ("the world is not all sparkly"), Emily listens to her own inner voice. She puts out all this effort to make the world more fair because it's the right thing to do. But she's also having a grand time doing it. For Emily, service is really fun.

Helping out in my community was just something I grew up with. For Girl Scouts, for instance, I would bring in items for canned-food drives, and I'd sort through my clothing for clothing drives for the needy. Whenever my elementary school had a food drive, I'd ask my mother for cans to bring in. My mom, in particular, has always been active. As a nurse, she knows a lot of the people who work in the cancer clinics. Whenever she'd hear of something that needed doing, she would do it, and I would help when I could.

The first time I knew it was time to do more than just contribute to someone else's cause was when I was in fourth grade, right after my grandma died. You need to understand that my grandma is really one of my heroes. Throughout my childhood, she told me stories about when she was younger. She was the last child born into a poor family in Appalachian Ohio with eleven or twelve kids. Her dad died when she was very, very young. Her mother had a hard time supporting the family. My grandmother would sit me down and tell me, "You're so lucky to have parents who can give you everything." When she was little, she'd wear the same dress to church for a year. She simply didn't have another one. And all the kids in her Sunday School class would make fun of her because of that. She said it was very embarrassing to her when she would walk down the street and be pointed out as, "Oh, she's one of the Belchers. They're poor." But kind neighbors would let her and her brothers and sisters come and pick fruit off their trees, and a few others helped her when she and her family needed it most.

When my grandma grew up, she got married, got a job, had three kids, and began saving money. Years and years later, when I was a little girl, she would take me with her to buy jackets and gloves and shoes out of her own pocket for the people in town who didn't have anything. She would say to me, "It wasn't fair for me, and so there's no reason anybody else should have to live through this too."

After she died, it finally sank in for me that she had done this—helping others—because somebody else had helped *her*. It hit me, like a click, "I get it now."

People can't help the family they're born into. If you're born into a family that's got $10 billion or a family that doesn't have a cent to its name, you can't help it if you're just a kid.

After my grandma's death, we spent some time in her town—it was the same one she had grown up in—and it was the first time I actually saw people who were poor. I had never really noticed before. Before, I thought everything was sparkly and perfect. My mother and I were buying some last-minute items for Thanksgiving—stuffing and vegetables—and there was a family in the aisle next to us buying baloney and bread for Thanksgiving with food stamps. They had a little kid running around without shoes. My grandmother's image came into my head, and a flash went off, and I thought, "Whoa!" As I got into the car, I was crying. "Mom, it's not fair," I said. "Can we give them something? Can we give them some money, or do *something?*"

Of course, my mother said we could do something, but that it might embarrass that family if we offered them money directly. She said that if I was bothered by what I saw, then I *had* to do something. She didn't say what, she didn't say when, she didn't say how. She just said, "Do something." All this time it was like a puzzle, and pieces were fitting in: Grandma telling stories, then her death, then me seeing poor people in stores. My mom saying "you have to do something" was the last piece of the puzzle. That's it! I'm going to have to buy stuff or raise money for people here in this poor town.

After the holidays, when we were back home and I was at a new school, I was still trying to figure out exactly what I would do. I couldn't get it out of my mind. I'd even write ideas down during study hall. Then my mother said she knew the addresses of some people who went to her high school and who had moved to Columbus and who might like to help. So that was how it began, with me writing about fifty letters to these people. It got to the point where I wasn't doing my homework in order to get this done. It was very important to me. It wasn't like anybody was forcing me to do this. I just thought, "This is the right thing." It was also a lot of work, and it was really hard. I thought, "It better be worth it. Somebody better respond or at least do something."

By this time it was November of the next year. Finally, I got some letters back with donations of money, some of them with $5 inside, some with $25. A few said, "This is such a great idea. Give me a call next year. I know some other people who might like to donate money." Every day when I came home from school, I'd ask my mom if I got any mail. When I did get mail, I'd say, "Yes!" That part was really exciting. I wrote thank-you letters to everyone who contributed. I even wrote to the ones who didn't respond, to let them know that people are responding to this appeal. Those letters didn't do any good, but that's how I learned what works and what doesn't.

At this point, things were sort of unorganized. I didn't have a definite plan yet. I only knew I wanted to call what I was doing Grandma's Gifts, to honor my grandma. First I wanted to open a bank account in the name of Grandma's Gifts, but when I only had about $250, the bank told me I didn't have enough to open an account. I said, "Excuse me? That isn't fair." I talked to the bank manager, who thought my idea was wonderful, and she added, "Next year, if you want to get some donations from us, just ask."

That taught me something. I'd never really realized how many people want to help but don't know how. It was hard to ask for money; it was sort of embarrassing. But people do want to help.

I knew that in my grandma's town there was a chain store, and that, as you walk in, there's a decorated Christmas tree with names hanging on tags. The tags say things like, "Little Suzie Jo would like so-and-so for Christmas." I asked the manager for some names off the tree. At the time, there were only three names left: two boys and a girl.

At first, I was more interested in helping the little kids, like most people. After all, little kids want all those toys that are such fun to play with. And the older kids aren't so adorable. But these kids were 11, 15, and 17, and when the manager read me what the kids wanted, I just sat down and said, "Wow." They weren't expensive things at all.

One kid wrote, "I've had the same pair of shoes for an entire year. I'd like a pair of shoes." He didn't even ask for a name brand. That's the kind of thing you just say to your mom, "Mom, my shoes have a hole in them." And you go out and buy a new pair. I kept thinking, "That's not even fair." The other boy wanted a model and a puzzle.

When the store manager got to the little girl's name, he said, "She doesn't care." What did he mean? She wrote, "Anything." This little girl had gotten to the point in her life where she couldn't ask for anything. It was like she was saying, "I don't really care what it is, as long as I can sit and open one present." It was so much worse than I had thought it was!

So I used the money I had to buy them some nice things that were on sale and that I found on clearance racks, because I knew they would like to have some of the same styles and brands me and my friends like. I got them clothes and books and lots of little things so they would have a lot of things to open. I got the little boy a card game I had loved.

After the holiday gifts were delivered that first year, I wondered what else I could do. I knew I wanted to continue asking for contributions so I could buy presents for more kids on the tree each year. I began by writing letters telling each of those who had contributed what I had bought with their money. I'd never really noticed how bad things were for some people. I think most people don't know, and that's one reason they don't help. This was a very emotional time for me. I was going home and people were telling me things that were so sad, and every day I'd feel like crying.

Then my mom read something in the paper about The Prudential Spirit of Community Awards, and I entered the contest, not expecting much. I figured at least I would have the satisfaction of just entering. When I got the letter saying I was one of the winners from my state, I was bouncing off the walls all day long. For weeks I got letters from people who had heard about the award and about my program. Some of them wanted to be added to the list to contribute next time. Then I got the $1,000 prize. I hadn't even known there was money involved!

All through this period, my parents were totally supportive. I tried to get some of my friends involved, but it didn't always happen. In eighth grade when this was mainly happening, it was hard. I'd say, "Guys, you wanna come help me?" And they'd say, "No, I can't, I gotta go home and watch TV." "Just for a little while?" "No, I can't. I've got sports practice." I'm *missing* it today so I can do this, I told them. Fine, then. And these were *good* friends.

Then my friends started hearing how I was getting mail every day about the award. They asked what it was for, and I told them it was for the stuff I'd asked for their help with and they'd said no. "Well, if you told me you could win a prize . . ." I told them the award wasn't the point. "Well, then what *is* the point?" To help somebody else. I had a long talk with my friends, and they finally understood what was going on.

One day I was standing outside a home-ec class when the teacher told the class they had to do a community-service project. Cool, I thought. Then when the kids groaned, she said, "You have to. It's part of your grade." What a thing to say! "You have to do this, it's not meant to be fun." That is *not* part of the community-service idea. That's just not right. It's *fun*.

If I could—I know this sounds funny—I'd find a way to make people see the light. By going places and seeing and hearing things that are just *not* supposed to happen. The world's not all it's cracked up to be, and people need to open their eyes.

I learned more than I ever expected to from doing Grandma's Gifts. First off, I discovered that life is not all that everybody says it is, because some people can't help what happens to them. It's just not *fair*. And then, when only ten out of the fifty letters got a contribution, I didn't think that was good. People need to be more aware. I wish more people would think, "Instead of throwing away those old clothes that don't fit, maybe I should put them in the drop box."

One of the biggest lessons I learned was to rely on myself, to listen to my feelings inside. And not to listen to all the hypocrites in the world who say, "That's stupid, that's a dumb thing. Sorry, I can't help you." Instead, I need to follow my own instincts about what needs to be done. This may sound insane, but everybody needs to sit and listen to themselves about what they think.

Grandma's Gifts has gone way beyond how it started a few years ago. On one past weekend alone, I collected over 1,000 pounds [454 kg] of canned-food items. I made Thanksgiving baskets to send to working families with children, and I sent baskets to a battered women's shelter in West Virginia. We've now been able to provide in excess of $200,000 in food, clothing, books, toys, and educational experiences to needy Appalachian kids. This includes the donation of more than 60,000 books which have been used to establish libraries in schools, health clinics, hospitals, Head Start facilities, community centers, and thousands of individual children's homes.

Beyond that, I've negotiated the support of nineteen corporations through grants, in-kind giving, and donation of goods and services. Through several national publicity opportunities, the support for Grandma's Gifts now comes from all across the United States. Last summer I built a web page for my project, and this exposure has allowed me to obtain the help of thousands of folks as well as mentor other people about how they can become active in their community. There is no other way to say it other than I have been incredibly blessed.

Once I picked up almost 50,000 pennies that a local elementary school had been collecting for Grandma's Gifts. Another time, two large boxes arrived on my front porch packed with toys from a family in Illinois who had read a magazine article about my work. Recently, Grandma's Gifts was able to fill a semi-truck with goods for Appalachia. This included food, clothing, books, and several sleighs full of goods for delivery by Santa on Christmas morning. This Christmas, Girl Scout troops, Boy Scout troops, schools, civic groups, and church groups have helped Grandma's Gifts in the Christmas Angel project.

It felt good that I was able to get my friends involved with the canned-food project, once they finally realized what I was doing. Also, people I've never met before are always coming up to me and offering their help. They say, "I saw an article about you, and I'd love to help you."

I've learned to respect people no matter how wealthy or poor they are, because everybody is equal. People take it for granted that their parents work their entire lives to support their kids. I don't take anything for granted. I could have been born into a less fortunate family.

Another thing I figured out is that there are different groups of people. In seventh and eighth grade, I had a good friend, but I never considered her one of my *best* friends until my other friends were off doing stuff that was just dumb. She agreed that the others were wasting their time, and instead joined me in volunteering. Now we're together all the time. I found that people that I relate to the best are the people who have the same frame of mind that I do.

Sometimes I would get discouraged when people didn't get it. I've had people read the flier I handed them at the supermarket entrance, look at me, and then laugh. One of the first fliers I handed out, this one lady had a snickery laugh. I said, "Mom, I cannot do this, I cannot do this!" This is not fair to me, and not fair to other people. And it's just not fair! But my parents were always there, reminding me, "Just keep going, it doesn't matter about them." Sometimes I get so excited about things and then nobody wants to help. That's the burnout point. You have to just personally do things that you enjoy, whether people approve of them or not. I would look back to my values and my family when I got discouraged.

As I've matured, I've grown in my ability to brush off those who doubt my intensity and drive. I am also very, very good at sniffing out people whose sole purpose to help is a tax deduction. But, overwhelmingly, my faith in mankind, and especially in kids, has been bolstered by meeting the people who have helped along the way.

Most of the people who helped me were like this one man who came out of a supermarket and said, "It's only a few cans, but I wish it could be more." Wow, that's so nice of people.

Grandma's Gifts will always be a part of me. I have a brother and sister who are 15-year-old twins. Next year, they will take a more active part in the operation of Grandma's Gifts.

One of my greatest dreams is to be able to establish an ongoing foundation for Grandma's Gifts. I want to be able to help bring the arts into the schools of Appalachia. When schools are worrying about heating their building or buying paper to write on, the arts become an afterthought. Music has played such an important and enriching part in my life, I want to share that beauty with my kids. I want them to know how it feels to squeeze wet clay through their fingers and manipulate that clay into a work of art—their own work of art. I want them to experience the way their feet will tap when they hear a Scott Joplin rag. I want them to be swept into the beauty of a Monet painting.

I have every faith that I can make this happen.

Brian Harris

CHAPTER 7

Brian Harris:

Getting to Know You

With an African-American father and a Caucasian mother, Brian Harris grew up particularly aware of racial issues. While he was still in mid-elementary school, Brian's whole family got involved in an inter-racial group, and he found himself evolving into a spokesperson for tolerance and understanding. Speaking out wasn't enough, however. Brian wanted to do more. Friendship Sees No Color is his extraordinarily successful pen-pal service that matched thousands of people of all ages with others of another race. The countless hours that Brian spent handling mail were worth every moment, he says, since it proved to him that the world is filled with good people who just need a little help figuring out how to make genuine contact with each other.

I was about 9 or 10 when my family joined an interracial group that would get together for picnics and outings. When newspaper reporters would come to do interviews with the adults, I would usually say something too. Because I was so young, they'd be particularly interested in what I would have to say. Soon, the group made me their youth spokesperson.

That meant I would go out with them to wherever they were having a conference or presenting a talk, and I would give speeches on what it was like to be young and biracial. Even before that, I had seen talk shows that focused on interracial families, and it seemed as though, inevitably, in every show, there would be someone who would bring up the topic of, "What about the kids?" And there would sort of be a negative slant to it, that the kids are going to suffer. When I got the opportunity to speak, I let people know that I was just like any of my friends.

Once I'd been doing speeches for quite a while, I was no longer only talking about being biracial, but incorporating larger insights about racism. My talks just kept developing. Then when I was in sixth grade, there were the Los Angeles riots. That was the point where I really recognized that things weren't as good as we'd like them to be. From my school, though it's in Orange County, not central Los Angeles, you could actually see smoke from the fires. That hit home.

I decided right then that I wanted to do something more. I started brainstorming to figure out what I *could* do. I would go over things in my head by myself, and then when I would come up with an idea, I would tell my parents about it and they knew if it was something I could do. I ran through different ways of bringing people together, but each idea had some fault or something that might keep it from being successful.

Finally, I settled on this idea for a pen-pal service called Friendship Sees No Color. I'd had pen pals before, and I knew that it was a nice way to communicate. And I knew it was an easy thing to do, that it didn't really require someone to fully come out of their comfort zone. It's still a little bit safe, especially when you're asking people to be connected with someone of another race. I knew that if I asked someone who lives in a very small town, without any exposure to people of other races, to suddenly meet someone of a different race, that might be a little bit too hard for them.

The pen-pal exchange seemed to be the perfect way of opening up lines of communication. My mom had told me that when she was younger she wished she had a black friend, since her own parents had always told her negative things about blacks. I hoped my project would offer an opportunity for young people, in particular, to make friends with people from different backgrounds.

From there it was a matter of getting the idea out into the world. Since I'd been around that interracial group, I'd learned that there are ways to get the media's attention. Most of my help came from my family, so far as preparing press releases and sending them out. I also sent letters to the morning talk shows. It was basically just me saying I'm a 12-year-old and I'm going to start this program. Then I waited to see what would happen.

I was lucky to have the producer of *The Home Show*, a popular morning show, call me. That was really exciting. The plan was that people would send in a stamped self-addressed envelope and an index card with all their information, their name, age, address, and race. Then I would find someone of one race and someone of a different race, both in the same age range, and put their index cards in each other's envelopes and send them off.

Within a month or so after appearing on that TV show, I had about 10,000 letters. It was pretty amazing and overwhelming. *The Home Show* invited me back a second time since they were so impressed by the response, and then after that there were probably another 5,000 letters within a month.

I also promoted Friendship Sees No Color by speaking at various universities and by appearing on numerous other television programs. Over the course of the next few years, the pen-pal service continued to bring in letters even after I stopped actively promoting it. It generated its own word of mouth. We totally lost count, but it's well over 20,000 people who joined.

At the time my younger brothers and sisters were a little too young, but me, my brother who's a year apart from me, and my mom and dad would sit down on weekends and spend some hours doing it. I would guess that over a four-year period, we put in many hundreds, even thousands, of hours. We're talking about letters coming from all over the country and eventually from all over the world, people from all different backgrounds. It was really neat to do. We'd go to the post office box every day and pick up crates of mail.

The main difficulty we had was that hundreds of people wouldn't follow the instructions to include a self-addressed stamped envelope. That was obviously a huge economic burden. One thing we did was sell T-shirts for Friendship Sees No Color. That was a popular idea and brought in about $100 we then used for envelopes and stamps.

I was lucky. I recognize that if I hadn't been this little 12-year-old trying to make a difference, it wouldn't have been as easy for me to sell the idea to the major media. And it was those TV shows that brought in the most applicants for pen pals.

My initial plan was for this to be strictly for young people, my age and around there. But once people started writing in and I got letters from many, many adults, I decided that, why not? If they want to do it, it's a *good* thing, not a bad thing. We ended up connecting as many adults as young people.

A lot of people have written to me saying, "Thanks, this really helped out." I got appreciative letters from 88-year-olds, 6-year-olds,

Americans, Jamaicans, Africans, Asians, Europeans, Christians, convicted killers, and everything else imaginable. One couple, both senior citizens, even ended up getting married!

My parents really helped me. They could easily have shot the whole thing down at the start. I didn't really get help from any friends. There were people who came in at times and tried to change things, who had these grand schemes for turning the project into a money-making thing, and that's not really what I wanted. It felt really good to do. I always believed you could make a difference if you tried, and this was proof for me. What this project also did was it helped give me more credibility for my speaking about racism and biracial issues. Before I started it, I would have to ask places to let me come and speak. And after, places would call me and ask me. Going out and giving presentations has always been my favorite kind of community service.

I did this from junior high all the way through high school. There were times at the start, with 10,000 letters in a single month to deal with, that were time-consuming. Obviously, being young, you feel like you want to go outside and play rather than work with the envelopes, but I think I got to play enough. I wouldn't dedicate *all* my time to the project. Still, I would try to stick with it. Anyway, I didn't look at it so much as work, because it was seeing everything that I wanted. It was hard for me to be resentful of it.

When I started this, I had no idea of the personal fringe benefits. When I applied to Stanford, their application is very interested in who you are and what you do, and things like community service really make you look a lot better. What they look for is dedication. If you're involved in one community-service activity that you stay with and you really care, they appreciate that.

Friendship Sees No Color has pretty much quieted down now. My little sister kept asking if she could do it. So at some point I might do a grand reopening and get it back out there. There are a lot of kids getting to writing age who weren't old enough at the time when I started the project. It would be great if they, too, could connect with kids of another race and see how similar we all are.

Obviously, I have the will to get out and do something and complete it, but I think anyone could have done what I did. Towards the end of high school, when I went to speak at junior highs and high schools, I would always try to let people know that one of the most important things is to get involved. Find a problem that concerns you and do something to help fix it. There's an amazing feeling of just knowing that you *are* doing something. I mean, you go to school and you do those usual things, and you get a sense of accomplishment when you get an A on a paper, but I think the feeling you get when you really know you're making a difference in people's lives or you're really helping to heal some sort of societal ill, that's a pretty big thing.

People have been dealing with the idea of racism for a long time, and I felt like, obviously I didn't eliminate racism and I never planned to, but the fact is that for 20,000-plus people, I at least did something. It's a really good thing to know you've been doing what you *should* do and you haven't just been complaining, which is easy to do.

CHAPTER 8

Anita Taylor:

"We Drive on That Road Every Day"

The death of a schoolmate in a hit-and-run accident was what motivated Anita Taylor to get involved. Like all accidents, it shouldn't have happened. If only there had been a sidewalk along that road! Anita took it upon herself to get a petition approved and a sidewalk constructed so that such accidents would be much less likely to happen in the future.

Sounds simple enough, but many people got involved, much time was spent, and, above all, the work had to be done in spite of the painful emotions it stirred up in everyone. From this single short-term community-service project, Anita learned a lot about life, people, and what it takes to get a government agency to take action.

When I was 12, J. D. Daniels, a boy who was a grade ahead of me, was walking along a busy road in Methuen, Massachusetts, with five of his friends on the way to his birthday party. A speeding car hit J. D. and threw him into the air. The driver sped off, and J. D. died within an hour.

I didn't know J. D. personally, but my younger brother and his younger sister were in the same class. I was devastated, as was the entire community. Not only was he someone from my school, Methuen Comprehensive Grammar School, but he was killed pretty close to home, about a mile away from our house, on our bus route. We drive on that road every day. When I heard about the accident, I couldn't control my sobbing. When my parents hugged me, it only made me think of the awful fact that J. D.'s parents would never be able to hug their son again.

My parents and I talked late into the night, and I used up a full box of tissues crying, before I came up with the obvious. It seemed that if there had been a sidewalk and if J. D. had been walking on it, he might still be here. The only problem was that there *was* no sidewalk on Washington Street. So why not put one there?

That night, I struggled to come up with a good opening statement for a petition. I typed up the front page and brought it into school on Monday morning. I didn't wait to find out any official way to do it—I just picked up the idea and ran with it.

When I went to J. D.'s classroom to get signatures, everybody was crying, both boys and girls. Everyone started signing the petition, kids and adults. We were trying to get as many signatures as possible before we turned in the petition at the Town Council meeting. Other kids and a lot of parents went around their neighborhoods getting signatures, too, and several teachers helped a lot. In exactly three weeks, we collected 820 signatures. Not a single person I went to turned me down for a signature.

I talked to my teachers and they arranged for the mayor and the Town Council chairwoman to come to my classroom and accept the

Anita Taylor

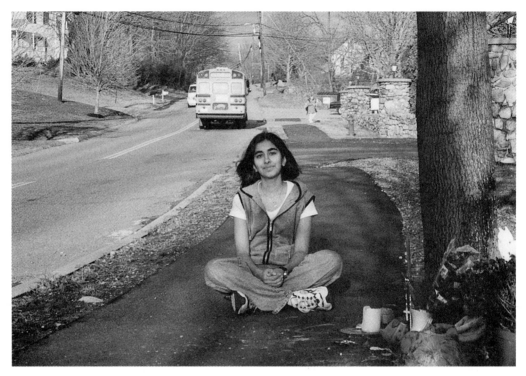

Anita Taylor worked hard to get this sidewalk built.

petition. I presented it to them, and it was arranged that I would present it to the entire Town Council at their meeting later that night.

That afternoon when I got out of school, my mom took me and my brother to J.D.'s house, where I gave his parents a copy of the petition. We all started crying. It was really emotional for all of us.

Later that evening, my family and I went to the Town Council meeting at the Town Hall. I stood at the podium and got ready to read the opening statement of the petition. I had so many butterflies in my stomach, but I knew I had to do this. I took a deep breath and started to read. After I finished, I walked up to the semi-circular assembly and handed them the petition. As I walked back, I could hear the applause from the audience. The council voted on the proposition and unanimously agreed. They said construction of a sidewalk would most likely begin in the spring of the following year.

A few months later, I called the Town Hall to find out what was happening with the sidewalk. I also called the Department of Public Works several times. They said they were backlogged with projects at the time, and that they would begin the sidewalk when they were caught up. After some complications with funding, the project finally began.

I learned that it really takes a lot of work to cause any change to happen. You really have to put your heart into whatever you're doing and spend lots of time doing it. Sometimes it was hard, because I had a lot of homework, but what kept me going was basically this feeling in the pit of my stomach every time we drove on Washington Street. J. D.'s family and friends had set up a little memorial by the tree for him with pictures, flowers, and small statues. Anytime you go past, you see the memorial by the tree and it reminded me of him, so you could say his memory kept me going.

I would do something like this again, but preferably under less tragic circumstances. I'm now involved in the community-service program at my school, Phillips Academy in Andover. Our school's motto is *No sibi,* which is Latin for "not for self," in which I really and truly and totally believe. We just recently had a party for one of our projects, in which we go into a nearby town and work with third-graders, helping them write. The community service I do with my school isn't required, but I do it because I like helping others and being with kids. It's also the sense of satisfaction that inspires me to help out. Because my parents help out in school and in soup kitchens sometimes, it seems natural for me to do it too.

I definitely got a sense of satisfaction out of doing this. The sidewalk is partially complete. They're doing it in phases, because construction still depends on funding from developments that are being put up. I learned, though, how to make the best come out of a bad situation. The sidewalk is going to make the neighborhood a lot safer for both children and adults.

My prize from Prudential was $1,000. I was really excited about that at first, but when I sat down and thought about it, it didn't feel quite right to keep it. I talked to my family about it, and we agreed that I should donate it. I gave half of it to the J. D. Scholarship Fund, to be awarded to a member of J. D.'s graduating class, and the other half to the school's drama club, which J. D. was actively involved in.

Even though we're still children, we really *can* change the world . . . a little bit at a time.

CHAPTER 9

Max Penning:

Hoops for the Hoopless

Playing basketball was Max Penning's passion. The Barrington, Illinois, fifth-grader played it on his driveway and on the playground at his suburban school. When he heard about a nearby Chicago school where the kids had no place to play his favorite game, he thought up a way to raise money to buy them hoops and more. "Save the world—eat pizza" became his motto for inspiring his pals, and it worked. Five months and 1,500 pizzas later, that inner-city school got its hoops, and Max and his friends got a new understanding of the world.

Max Penning

Even before I started my hoops project, I had already learned how good it feels to help somebody. When I was littler, I used to collect cans for food drives at my school and church. But it was quite different to start something big on my own, much more work—but more rewarding too.

I live in a suburb of Chicago. My church, which is Lutheran, had been helping Holy Family Lutheran School, a small private school in Chicago, about forty-five minutes away. Most of the kids lived in Cabrini Green, a housing project, and their parents sent them to that school to get them out of their high-crime neighborhood. My friends had been members of the church longer than we had, and they discovered this school and told us about it. At that school, the students didn't have enough money for learning equipment. So our church was giving them money, and a lot of people were volunteering at the school. We'd look in the church bulletin and see notices for "volunteers wanted." Me and my family would go to the school and play with the kids and help out. We read to the kids, and helped them edit the stories they had written. This was in late fifth grade, early sixth grade.

On my first visit to the school, I especially noticed that they didn't have much of a playground. It was just a 10-by-10-foot [3.05-by-3.05 meter] blacktop. And they didn't have any playground equipment. I learned that they didn't have hoops at home either, because they lived in city apartments, not suburban homes. Since I enjoyed playing basketball so much, I decided I wanted to get them basketball hoops.

Someone had recently sold us some very good pizzas as part of a fund-raiser. I looked up the phone number on the box and asked my mom to find out if we could sell those pizzas also. Then I wrote a letter to the fifth-grade boys' and girls' basketball team at my school and explained about the need for hoops and how we could sell these pizzas to make money to buy equipment. We had a meeting at school, and I knew the kids weren't going to sell pizza unless they liked them, so we gave away free pizza to the kids at the meeting. A lot of kids wanted to get involved once they tasted the pizza and heard about the school's needs. About 100 kids got involved in selling the pizzas.

We bought the pizzas—which come three to a kit and you heat them yourself—for $8 and sold them for $14, so we made $6 on each box. We sold those to everyone in my neighborhood and at my school. I called people, and then I'd go to their doors. I put a notice up at my church and my school.

Most of my friends whom I've known since kindergarten got involved too, plus all my friends down the street. I started the project and got the credit, but there were about twelve friends in it with me. Some of my friends' parents helped; some of the church members helped. It just seemed to happen—I didn't need to beg anyone to help. My brother helped by getting his church confirmation class to sell pizzas. My gym teacher advised us on what equipment to order. My mom was like my partner—she would make a lot of calls, and she'd take me and my friends over to the school.

Though we had schedules and goals of how much we wanted to sell, it was actually kind of informal. Whenever we would get together, not necessarily once a week, or whenever we saw each other, we talked about the project. We sold pizzas once a month to different businesses, and we sold some at an antique show. We sold them door to door. We would set up a truck somewhere with all the pizzas and they'd just come and buy them. The person who supplied the pizzas often helped us too.

My mom usually dealt with the money. We'd send in an order form for the equipment, and the stuff would be sent to the school. From the first sale, I was able to buy them six hoops and six balls. My grandma later paid for a shed for the school where we kept everything.

We had several separate sales over the life of the project. Some people would reorder every month. Then, so the project could continue without so much time on my part, my mom made an arrangement with the local Volunteer Center. She agreed to be on their board if they would adopt this project. So from then on we split the profits with the Volunteer Center. Later, one company bought $3,000 worth of pizza, some for every employee, and all the proceeds went to the school to fund a swim-and-gym program. We made $9,000 altogether, and the Volunteer Center is still selling those pizzas.

There were hard times. My two best friends always helped, but sometimes my other friends didn't want to come over and make the phone calls. They wanted to go to the school we were helping and play with the kids—the fun part. I would have to ask them more than once, and in the end they would usually say yes. During the school year, I'd make time for homework and for this. I'd have to give up time playing with my friends, but since a lot of the time my friends would be doing it with me, I wasn't really missing anything.

Maybe I'm a little more self-confident than some of those who didn't get this involved. I can start something, and I can actually get it finished. It was hard at first to call people, but then I got used to it and knew how to do it. I also learned how to speak in front of groups.

I'll always remember one part in particular. Several of us went to the school to sort and set up their equipment, pump the balls, and put the field-hockey equipment together. It was like Christmas for those kids. They had never seen jump ropes with handles on them. Then I organized a baseball game, and I pitched a ball to an older boy. On his first swing, he hit the ball over the school, where it flew out of sight. I was so excited to share in these kids' happiness. You get a good feeling at the end when a project is completed.

Jenny
Hungerford

CHAPTER 10

Jenny Hungerford:

From Down and Out to Speaking Out

To understand Jenny Hungerford's remarkable contribution to her Wisconsin community and beyond, you have to begin with her sad attempt at age 11 to make friends with a group of smokers—friends who turned out to be really bad news. So many horrors followed over the next few years, it's truly a wonder Jenny survived at all. And yet, there's a happy ending. Anyone hearing her story, a story she travels all over to share so that others may be saved from what she went through, is bound to think twice before making the same mistakes. She tells it best in her own words.

When I was 11, I had a hard time making friends. We had just moved, and though I'd never had trouble making friends before, I felt awkward and unattractive at this age. I felt like my teeth were too big and that I was anything but pretty. So when I saw some kids smoking, I decided that if I went up there and asked them for a cigarette, that for at least the time it took to stand there with them and smoke that cigarette, I'd have "friends."

It didn't take long before that group introduced me to other kids, and eventually I started drinking and getting high with all of them. Within a not-very-long period of time, I made the drugs and the alcohol my friends. A couple of years later, I began using cocaine too.

The first time I ran away was when I was 13. I had been late coming home and my mother saw me in a car, and I wasn't allowed to ride in cars, and I was messed up at the time from drugs, so I decided not to go home. From that point on, for the next year and a half, I ran away about twenty-three times. I got caught every time, but I never stayed home more than twenty-four hours. I was mostly afraid of not being able to use the drugs anymore if I stayed home.

When I ran away, I went anywhere to stay warm. I stayed at friends' houses for a while until their parents started to catch on to what was going on. So eventually I started staying by myself or with other kids. I'd sleep in basements of apartment complexes if I needed to, to keep warm. A lot of the time I was outside.

During that time, my mom tried putting me in treatment centers to find out what was wrong. She didn't know I had a drug and alcohol problem. She only knew I was running away, and she didn't know why. There are only three reasons why a runaway runs away: drug and alcohol abuse, physical or sexual abuse in the home, or intense family conflict in the home. As far as she knew we had none of those things going on.

Eventually, after completing my first treatment-center program, when I was 13½, I did tell her. That first treatment helped a little.

I would stay home for maybe a couple of weeks at a time. It was just that I kept relapsing and relapsing. I was having a lot of problems in school too, of course, but I kept the mail from my mom so she never knew all of what was going on. Finally she quit her job to totally dedicate herself to helping me.

I went through three short-term treatment-center programs, each one lasting only about eleven to fourteen days. Each time, I was always very sincere about wanting to quit, but I didn't know how. I didn't have enough time in those brief programs to learn the skills I needed to live a life without the drugs. By then, my self-esteem was so low that I was battling with eating disorders too.

When I was 14½ years old, I had been going through intense counseling, and my mom decided I needed a long-term treatment. In this state, at 14, you're allowed to legally deny medical treatment. So when my mom wanted to put me into a six- to nine-month treatment program, I refused. My mom and I had to go to court, and we battled it out there. Everybody was on her side of the courtroom: my social worker, my counselor, and my probation officer (I had a probation officer because, much earlier than all this, I'd been in jail for running away and for stealing a van with two other runaways). And then there was me alone on my side.

You can't imagine what a hard time that whole period was for me. During that time I was physically and sexually abused by people who were supposed to be friends. I was always in a state of mind where I was nearly comatose. That was how I used drugs: I wouldn't stop until I couldn't do anymore. For a long time, I couldn't talk about it.

I hit a lot of bottoms. One was when I overdosed on peyote. I had tripped for five days straight before they finally got me into a hospital. I spent the last day of the hallucinating in restraints. I didn't even know what had happened.

I wanted things to start getting better, but I didn't know how to turn my life around. I had gotten to the point where I thought

Jenny Hungerford's story has helped many other teenagers turn their lives around.

suicide was my only option. I didn't want to live that life anymore. I really was sick of it. My mom saw all this in me, and I didn't. I didn't see how another treatment center would help.

In the courtroom my mom educated the judge about what I'd done. He didn't know kids could be addicts. She told him about all the things I'd done that could have killed me, should have killed me. So the judge got me into a treatment center the next day. And I haven't gotten high since that day, five and a half years ago.

At the center, it was like a big family. We went to school half days, and we had intensive counseling. I had been using cocaine heavily by then, so I went through withdrawal there.

I met a girl who wanted to quit. She was my age, and she showed me it was possible. She kept telling me, "Help me and I'll help you." I'm almost ready for tears right now talking about this. She helped me more than anyone. Having a peer say, "Hey, you can do this"—that was what made me decide I wanted to do it.

There was another important influence on me after that. At a Narcotics Anonymous meeting, a woman stood up and started to talk about what was going on in her life. I remember watching her and thinking that the woman glowed. It was like nothing I could describe, I didn't even have a word for it. I just remember that she glowed. Everything about her life was okay. Even the parts she wasn't happy with, the parts she was crying about, they were all normal parts of life, and she was living life on life's terms. I found out later that the word was serenity. I remember looking at her and thinking, "I just want to be a little bit shiny. I don't need to glow, I just want to shine just a little bit." That was the date I decided that I was going to do everything in my power to live my life and be a little bit shiny.

When I got out of that treatment center, which had felt safe, my mom moved us out of the area where all these people knew me. I was turning 15. Still, since a couple of girls knew my past, everyone soon knew it. I was in that same position with no friends that I'd been in when I was 11. Though I went to Narcotics Anonymous meetings, that was probably the hardest time of any, and now I didn't have the crutch of using drugs.

But I was so determined to make a go of it that I sought help from my guidance counselor. I explained to her what my life had been like before, and I told her I might need help, because I still didn't trust myself. And she asked me to do a presentation, to speak to fifth- and sixth-graders and tell them my story. I'd never spoken in front of people. She said, "Yes, but I think you'll do okay, and I want you to do this." And she ended the conversation.

I was really scared about it. I asked my mom to do it with me. We sat one night and talked about what we were going to say to these elementary-school kids. We had the first heart-to-heart we'd had since I was about 10½ years old.

So we went to the school, and we did two presentations, two days in a row. And it made the front page of all the newspapers. After that, we had schools calling us. I was in awe. I couldn't believe that all these people wanted me to come and talk, considered me somebody who could help them.

In turn, doing the presentations boosted my self-esteem to the point where I didn't *want* to do drugs anymore. I wasn't even thinking about them anymore. I just wanted to help other people. I realized that I might be able to save someone's life or prevent another teen from starting an addiction, if only I were willing to take the risk of sharing the most painful experiences of my life.

We did a lot of presentations in our area, and we would never take money for doing them. Eventually we started speaking at treatment centers. I started having kids call me to share their stories, and some told me that I was a person who shined. That I glowed. That was the best part.

Eventually, we started working with Wisconsin Association for Runaway Services, providing a series of alcohol and other drug abuse and runaway prevention activities in Wisconsin, Illinois, and Delaware. They'd provide the funds I needed to speak to larger groups, and I'd do fund-raisers for them. We started doing a series of scenes, called "Jenny: A Day in the Life of a Teenage Addict," which is a reenactment of the night I overdosed on peyote. We often have question-and-answer sessions after my dramatizations. We include teens from the audience in the presentations whenever we can. I also give keynote addresses about the importance of positive peer pressure and role modeling.

We're hoping to get funds this year for a drama troupe that performs true-life experiences. We have lots of people saying, "I've got this story, I'd like to share it." No acting skills needed, as it's all from the heart.

There was a lot of work involved at each stage of the project. For the reenactment, a script had to be written, stage hands and volunteer actors had to be recruited, and rehearsals had to be held. Then there were props to be gathered, promotional materials to be produced and distributed, matching funds to be found, and thank-you's and other follow-ups to be completed. And anytime I would be away from school, I had to plan ahead, do homework ahead of time, and take tests early. Not easy!

I did go through a stage where I was giving eight or nine presentations a month, and I was missing too much school. It did get really hard, though my grades were still up. I learned to slow it all down or I'd have burned out. We never say no to people, but instead we try to spread out the scheduling of the programs. Sometimes we have to schedule them a year later.

One odd thing was the kind of celebrity status I was acquiring among my peers, especially since I began getting media attention. A lot of teens were looking at what had happened in my life as, "Oh, you had complete freedom." I didn't want them to romanticize it that way. I didn't have any boyfriends or any friends at all during that whole bad time. All I had were associates, people you use to keep warm when you're sleeping out on the sidewalk. It scared me that anyone might get the wrong message from my experiences. I even decided to turn down some national television appearances, for fear their goals weren't the same ones as mine, but were only to get high ratings.

Our main message is that you don't know if you're going to become an addict when you try that first fix. I did not know when I took that first cigarette that it was going to lead to the life I had. "Just say no"—I agree with that. But an easier bit of advice is, "Wait to make that decision until you're older. Wait until the legal drinking age. You really don't need it, it's not going to make things better in your life." I've never met anyone whose life has been made better by alcohol or drugs.

As for those so-called old friends of mine, I know a few of them have died. Most of them are still living that life. As sad as that makes me, I'm so happy I'm not there anymore.

What did I learn about myself? That I'm worth what my mom put into saving me. I always thought I was nobody. And I know I can make a difference now, and I know that every person can. That one person can change and help so many people, because I've learned that I can be that person now, and I'm strong enough to be that person.

One of the more memorable moments in all this was when a suicidal teen asked me for help. Another was seeing my mom's face when I was honored as a "hero" at a prevention conference.

I'm excited about life now. I look forward to my future and all the healthy things that come with life that I didn't think I'd experience. I always believed I was going to die the next time I used drugs. Going from that to "Someday I'd really like to have kids, family, and a career," is a wonderful feeling. Now I know I can have those things.

CHAPTER 11

Michael Harris:

"This Land Is My Land. . . ."

A self-described "country boy" from the tips of his boots to the tires on his truck, Michael Harris had his first small herd of cattle—four cows—by the time he was in eighth grade. Even earlier, beginning in third grade, the Arapaho, Oklahoma, native made a deep connection to the land his family has lived on for four generations. Yet as he roamed the terrain of Custer County, Michael could see the ugly effects of pollution beginning to take its toll.

Michael began a community-service project that continued at full strength under his leadership for at least a decade. Besides cleaning up the countryside, his main goal was to educate young people about the importance of recycling. He also helped teach many thousands of individuals to care as much as he does about what happens to the land people too often take for granted.

Michael Harris

I love to camp, hunt, fish, run my horses all through the pastures, and hang out in the country. I live on the edge of town, but my family owns about 20 acres [8.04 hectares] of land. We lease some land too, though the amount varies from year to year. I know all the farmers in the county, and I ask them for permission to fish on their land. They usually give it. I know everyone around here, and I got to know all the land, too, when I was still very young.

When I was 9, I joined 4-H, and in eighth grade, which was as soon as I could, I got involved in Future Farmers of America (FFA). I started Environmental CPR (Concern, Preserve, and Reserve) that first year in 4-H and continued it all through high school, when I turned it over to another kid.

I have a strong love for the outdoors. I'm not fond of cities with their pollution and smog. My mom's the county clerk, which makes her a county politician, and so I learned a lot about the issue of pollution at an early age. We live only an hour and a half from Oklahoma City, and I could see the pollution of a big city for myself. But there's lots of pollution out in the country too. When you see trash on the side of the road, it's just plain ugly. I could see the depletion of our resources firsthand, and I began to realize the environment needs resuscitation.

When I was thinking about what project to get involved in, I decided it had to be the environment. My mom was very supportive of everything I did in 4-H, and she'd give me an emotional boost before giving a speech when I was only 9 years old—and shy.

My project started out pretty small scale. Wildlife is a big part of the environment. So for a start, I gave speeches to educate people about wildlife and Mother Nature through 4-H, at county speech contests, and to little kids wherever I could. And then the project grew as I got older. Its aim is to conserve all natural resources, including water, soil, plants, wildlife, and people. The ripple effect of all this activity has extended to the whole state of Oklahoma and

Michael Harris's work for the environment has had an impact in his community.

beyond. We got the help of area schools and local government agencies. I figure CPR has reached more than 460,000 people.

A big part of Environmental CPR the first few years was collecting and recycling more than 22,000 pounds [9,980 kg] of landfill material over a four-county area. Here's what was collected and recycled thanks to the efforts of CPR and a lot of volunteers: 724 evergreen trees, 11,000 pounds [4,990 kg] of office paper and newspaper, thousands of greeting cards and stamps, more than a ton of aluminum, a couple thousand telephone books, nearly 1,000 pounds [454 kg] of clothing, and 500 pounds [227 kg] of glass and plastics.

Then as I started getting older, I got over my fear of public speaking and I started doing more of it. By the time I applied for the Prudential award, I had given twenty-two workshops, thirty-two speeches, set up thirty-seven educational displays, written fifty-four articles, done twenty-one radio promotions, and presented seventeen programs. When I work with preschoolers and early-grade students, I use puppets and videos. Workshops, speeches, displays, and articles reach large audiences of older kids and adults.

Environmental CPR was one of the two clubs I set up. The other was called CUE Club (Clean Up Environment), and it was for fourth- through sixth-graders. We'd have monthly meetings, take a field trip each year, and I'd produce a newsletter, which was sent to the kids every month. Even when I was in high school and got very busy with sports, I continued the newsletter to keep the kids aware of environmental issues at all times. The newsletters contained an environmental calendar and motivating tips and ideas. We'd put in simple things like "Shut off the water when you're brushing your teeth," for the very youngest kids, and "Don't throw your paper out the car window." There were environmentally based puzzles and riddles. We tried to keep their interest by making this fun. I know that you have to get kids early to teach them the impact they can have on their environment and why that's so important. By the time people grow up, they've gotten lazy, and their habits are hard to change.

Once when we took a field trip to a water-treatment plant at a nearby lake, the kids got bored by the explanation that was given them. I like kids a lot and have fun with them, so I said, "Let's go to the beach," and we grabbed plastic bags and started picking up trash. We made a game out of it and ended up filling a whole truckload of trash. Who can find the most wrappers? Who can find the biggest item? One kid found a tire.

I also did a lot of radio shows, giving my environmental spiel over the air. People who heard of my winning 4-H county awards would call and let me do that. I was a youth educator for the state of Oklahoma.

CPR put large bins out to collect Christmas trees for recycling. Then we chopped them up and used them as small animal shelters. A television station heard of that and came out and did a story on it.

Another activity was getting involved in working with the Evergreen Clubhouse, a clubhouse dedicated to retraining those who have fallen on hard times. Really deprived individuals and even homeless people could come in and do an afternoon's work and get a little money for food. What CPR did was set up large cardboard bins in Clinton and Arapaho, Oklahoma, like at the county courthouse, where they use a lot of office paper. The Clubhouse workers would then sort the paper and pack it so it could be sent to a recycling place. The money from selling the paper helps defray part of the cost of running the Clubhouse.

We put bins for Christmas cards and used telephone books at the post office and at my school and at grocery stores. I advertised them with fliers and once with an ad in the newspaper, plus I did my radio plugs for the recycling efforts. The greeting cards were sent to a hospital in San Antonio for children with cancer.

The used postage stamps that we got people to recycle were sent to bedridden veterans for collections and also to a club called "Poor Children of Puerto Rico Club," where they were to be used as a teaching aid for history, science, and English.

In my senior year, I got a grant of about $500 from the Department of Environmental Quality, and I used it to fill three trunks with games and environment-related objects. I brought them to three elementary schools. That way, though I wouldn't be around to continue the project, I knew the teachers would go on and teach environmental consciousness for at least a few minutes each week.

Getting the transportation we needed for all that recycling was one of the hardest parts. Fortunately, the county commissioner was very helpful with this on the county level, as were family and club members on the local level.

An ongoing challenge was the apathy of the public over the fact that our natural resources are in danger. There were times I wanted to throw in the towel. My mom was always there for me, always pushing me to build my better self. She got me to where I could get in front of a large audience. I didn't have many friends my age, just three or four of us country boys who hung together. But they were always working, so this was my project. The best part of winning the award was when, during the ceremony, I finally got a chance to give my mom the credit she deserves.

It sounds like I did a tremendous amount of work on all this, and I did, but on average it took about ten hours of my time a month. That's only one less day per month to be a couch potato!

Now I'm an animal science/ranch operations major. My goal is to be a cowboy and manage a large ranch and get paid for it. Buying your own land is so expensive. And I'd live on the ranch and raise a family.

I've learned more than I can say from this project, and I advise all young people to consider volunteering their efforts. I learned leadership, how to coordinate projects, how to communicate with a variety of people, and the ability not to become discouraged. I also made a lot of memories and many new friends. The many awards I won were high points, providing me with incentive to work even harder, and giving me a great chance to promote CPR and its goals.

Sometimes you need to go against the grain. When you're doing community service, what you're doing might not be what people think is cool, but the right thing isn't always the coolest thing. I knew this was the right thing because I grew up in the country and when you see what's happening to the environment, it's just ugly, it's not right. You've got to respect the land. To me, the motivation was simply, "This *has* to be changed."

Kristen Deaton

CHAPTER 12

Kristen Deaton:

C'mon, Play Ball— Anyone Can!

Think about what a natural part of youth it is to walk onto a baseball field and take up a position. It matters less how good you are than that you're playing ball on a team of your classmates. Now imagine never ever having had such an experience. Kristen Deaton, who played softball with great enthusiasm all her life, decided she would open up that everyday pleasure to kids in wheelchairs, on crutches, and with every possible kind of physical challenge.

Anyone Can Softball is a softball league for young people with special needs. Kristen matched kids with able buddies, arranged locations, uniforms, coaches, tickets—all the details that make a game happen—and then had her many hours of hard work and devotion amply rewarded. The sight of these kids finally enjoying what comes so easily to others—and getting to see it again and again—has given Kristen deep gratitude for the role she was lucky enough to play. She thinks she's gotten more out of her project than anyone.

I grew up in a school district that encouraged community service, whether it was helping at Thanksgiving with a canned-food drive or coat drives in the winter. As a class representative in elementary school, I got hands-on experience early. Whatever my school offered, I did it.

Once you see a need—whether the need is food for the hungry or a doll for a little girl who doesn't have one or recreational opportunities for people with disabilities—you look for a way to help out with that need. At least that's how I've always felt. Once when my parents asked me what I wanted for my Christmas present, I said, "More hours in the day!" They said, "You'd fill them up anyway." Yes, I would.

When you find fulfillment in something, you continue to do that. For some, it's athletics, which I love too. For some, unfortunately, it's going out and partying. Getting involved and helping is where I find fulfillment; that's where my heart is happy. I look for that. I can feel warmth in my heart when I serve others.

It's actually easier for me when I get to turn away from myself and what I need in this world and turn towards what others need. It brings a reality to my world. The most important thing in this world is not winning a scholarship or getting straight A's. It's finding out who we are as people and helping one another to do the very best we can. I was lucky enough to find that fulfillment at a younger age than some, and that's where my commitment to community service started.

Anyone Can Softball evolved out of the intersection of my mom's career and my own sports interests. My mom is a pediatric physical therapist, and I grew up going to work with her. I always interacted with her patients during their therapy sessions, whether she met them in their homes or they came to her office. They responded to me just because I was another child. I also found ways to help. Really, for me, though, it was just playtime.

I started playing softball when I was 5 years old. As I was getting older and talking about the tournaments my friends and I were going to, I'd still go to work with my mom. We'd gotten close to the families, and we'd invite them out to my games. But the most I or my teammates would ever do for these little girls or these little boys who could not play themselves was to sign a softball and say, "Hey, thanks for coming."

I have a picture in my head of me standing on the field with my team watching a little girl named Taylor Telford roll off in her wheelchair with her family. They had come to many of my games. My mom's been Taylor's therapist since she was a baby, and Taylor, who has cerebral palsy and is vision-impaired, is only two years younger than me.

One Sunday afternoon my mom and I were just kind of sitting there at the kitchen table, talking about life. I don't remember exactly how that conversation went, but we came up with this idea of a way to do something special for kids like Taylor. And we both said, "Why not?" I was 16 and I had the contacts within the softball arena, knew the commissioner of the local ballpark, and my mom had the contacts within the pediatric special-needs community.

Our initial goal was to find about ten or twelve kids to form a T-ball team at an exhibition game. The interest turned out not to be for that, but for a league. That spring we had seventy-two people signed up to play, divided into four teams. It was staggering.

I'm much more of a talker than my mom, so I went out on the trail for buddies—assistants to the players on the field. A buddy is used to bring each one of the players to the exact same playing level. A child who has attention deficit disorder may be able to hit the ball and run but may need a lot of verbal commands. So the buddy would say, "We're going to pick up the ball and we're going to throw it there," or "We're going to run to first base." Whereas with a child who's severely handicapped in a wheelchair and can't move his hands, the buddy will pick up the ball for him, let him feel the ball and let him know that he's a part of the play by saying, "Okay, we're going to throw it to first base now."

So my mom would set up meetings, and I'd come and speak to different groups: Boy Scout groups, church groups, other softball teams, other high schools. We were able to round up sixty buddies to start.

Our rules state that any child who is not able to play in a "normal" league is able to play in my league. We have children in wheelchairs, on crutches, and with a wide variety of special needs.

A lot of these parents never had an opportunity to be part of a team. We helped them decide on team colors and team uniforms and the scorekeeper and the head coach, and the dugout mom and who was going to do drink tickets, from the littlest details on up.

Besides players and buddies, we also had to get the facilities. Our local ballpark's fields were not wheelchair accessible. The owner decided to do the required renovations himself without taking money from a sponsor. My mom and I got together and we took ASA's (Amateur Softball Association) T-ball rules and modified them to our needs, and we got sanctioned as a league.

So we got the rules, we got the park, we got the players, we got the buddies, and they got their uniforms and their gloves. It was just amazing; people have such wonderful hearts. As many people as we had who couldn't afford the league fees, we had *more* people say that they could help. Our commissioner was also very helpful.

The only people who were unhelpful were the media, and that was only at the very beginning. We tried *so hard* to get coverage. We only wanted them to help spread the word. Our first write-ups were actually letters from parents writing to their local papers thanking my mom and me. Once it spurred the media on, they went nuts. At the end, we had two of the four major TV stations come out. They've been extremely helpful ever since.

Certainly, there were moments of frustration, and there were moments of stress. At times, we had papers everywhere, we didn't know what we were doing, my mom and I were just two little people. . . . To try to keep things in order, we made ongoing lists. I remember different piles and stacks of paper. With the buddies, as much as you hate to do this, each of the parents has to sign a waiver of liability. All those registration forms!

We had *some* help. Some of my close friends coached a team, and they're still doing it three years later. It's a little unusual, but they love it. One of my high school teachers was very instrumental in getting buddies for us. But helpers weren't nearly as consistent as we were. Nobody was ever very negative about the program and all the efforts I was putting into it, but they'd say, "How can you do this? *Why?*" What I used to answer then was just, "Because." Whenever I think or feel something is right, that it should be done, that's what I do. So it was just kind of, "Because. That's what I do. That's what I like. That's what I want to do, it's what's fun to me."

I've come to the realization that my mom and I were two very inexperienced people. We didn't have the time, we didn't have the energy, resources, knowledge, anything. There's no way we could have done it. When we look back, we wonder, "How is this in existence?" The project was continually blessed. We're lucky that we get to experience it.

That first season, we got to have our finals at the National Softball Hall of Fame in Oklahoma City, at the most gorgeous field in the world, with this huge scoreboard and great sound system. The kids got to see their names up in lights.

Four years later, there are ten teams. We have a little over 170 players. The majority are ages 4 to 24, with a few older. We split them last year into an upper and a lower division. Anyone Can Softball has a life of its own now. It would continue without me. That's something we worked really hard to establish. My brother did a lot of paperwork and day-to-day stuff when I left for college. And he organized the tournament we just had. We're also striving to expand it to Anyone Can Sports, to bring in a basketball league, a soccer league, a bowling league.

I may go into pediatric physical therapy as a career, but I'm not certain. I've always said I want to be happy, have a family, and change the world. I'm just not sure how yet.

When starting community service, I had no clue that you could get awards for it, and scholarships! You get paid to do this?!

I've gotten letters from people in other states who wanted to copy Anyone Can. I got together hard copies of all the information I had, and put together a how-to packet and sent them out. I know of one league that is thriving in Indiana, called "The Challenger League." I remember this so clearly: I got a thick packet one day from Indiana, opened it up, and started flipping through these newspaper articles and pictures. I thought, "These aren't 'my' kids, but they're playing Anyone Can." And I started crying. Is that real, are there people somewhere else playing? And I was like, wow—to see people I don't know benefiting from what I've done.

The kids love the game. They've never been allowed to do this before. They've never had their own uniform, with their own team, their own colors, with their number on their uniform. It's not an honorary uniform; it's theirs that they wear to play.

It's neat for me to see my kids who started off originally in walkers because they couldn't even walk by themselves at all, now walking by themselves. We have so many stories of the kids who stand taller because of this.

As amazing as it is for the kids, there are the parents. To see their child on the field, something they've never seen before . . . Tears in their eyes, ohmigosh. They thank us. But it's very hard for me to accept thanks. Maybe we opened up a door, maybe we provided an opportunity, but their child is the one out there doing it.

Another thing is how the project has affected the buddies. Our key target area for buddies has been high school age. I have people in high school that I go talk to and prepare, and they just don't know what to do at first. They say they're a little nervous, a little apprehensive, and they say, "I don't know if I'm going to be talking too young or too old. I don't know how or when I should help." So I would talk them through it, and talk to their parents. I mean, five minutes later, five minutes after the game started, they realized the buddy wasn't helping the player play, it was a group effort. It was the buddy and the player playing the game together. Instead of looking at a child who has a disability, they now saw a friend. And so this was able to break a lot of social barriers, amazingly quickly. You're interacting so intensely. It's just you and the child at this position. They come up to me and they thank me, and I say, "You did it." I'm so thankful that some people have had the opportunity to break through that barrier. Before, maybe they were seeing the wheelchair instead of the person, whereas *now* they see that there's somebody there.

People ask if I would do it again. It's been a long haul. But when you see that little girl or that little boy coming across home plate in a wheelchair, with that smile on their face, with their eyes shut, with their hands in the air, and you see the stands just going crazy, and that child knows the applause is for them, for nobody else in the entire world but for them, and they've never experienced that before—to see that just one time—I mean, I'm so blessed, I've seen it hundreds, maybe thousands of times now—but to see it one time, I would do it all over again.

I've learned more from these kids, and I've gained more from these kids than I think that I'll ever be able to gain from anything else in my life.

Tyrell Nickens

CHAPTER 13

Tyrell Nickens:

The Happy Faces of Ty's Friends

From the time Tyrell was a toddler, he spent time around his mother's caseload of mentally handicapped people. As he grew older, many of these individuals became his special friends. Tyrell loved making them happy and seeing their smiles. When he was 11, he founded Ty's Friends Xmas Fund to raise money to buy gifts and to coordinate a huge party for the clients in his mom's caseload and beyond.

From one simple desire—to see more of his special friends enjoying a holiday party—Tyrell's project just grew and grew until hundreds of gifts are now distributed each year, with recipients coming from all counties in this part of Virginia. Tyrell himself learned the skills of getting help from others and speaking out on behalf of those in the community who are less able to do so themselves. After all, what are friends for?

When I was 8, my mother, who's a case manager for persons with mental handicaps, had this big party at the end of the year to celebrate all the volunteers who had helped her make their lives easier in one way or another. I helped wrap and give out gifts. I was the youngest person who was helping, and I got a certificate and a gold key for volunteering.

My mom's job used to sponsor Christmas parties for her clients, but the agency's budget got so low that the parties and Christmas gift-giving stopped when I was 11. None of the adults had gotten Christmas gifts anyway, only the children, and I felt that it wasn't fair. I've always been lucky enough to have a lot of things, and my parents always encouraged me to share. So I said to my mother, "I'm going to take this Christmas party on myself, and begin a fund for it." I called it Ty's Friends Xmas Fund.

My mom thought it was great that someone my age would think about doing something like this. Both my mother and my father helped me a lot. I've been doing it ever since.

I began by writing letters to all the area businesses, like fast-food places and video stores, soliciting funds so we could buy the gifts ourselves and then wrap and deliver them on Christmas Eve. I also wrote letters to the editor of our local newspaper and to the churches in our area. The gifts were for longtime clients in my mom's caseload, mentally handicapped people who I grew up knowing, and who became my friends.

Some of the young people in my church youth ministry helped me wrap the gifts, and we wrapped over 100 gifts in one night. It was fun. They said, "I'd like to do this again." The next year, instead of just wrapping gifts, they got to come to the party and have fun there too.

I don't see myself as any different from my friends who haven't started projects like this. I see myself as just raised that way, because my parents always helped different people. My mom and dad volunteer on the local rescue squad as EMTs [emergency medical technicians]. They take their equipment to local schools and fairs to show kids of all ages what they do, how the equipment works, and how to prevent injuries and that sort of thing.

Each time a letter from me to the editor was published, a lot of people in the community would write and say they had a lot of items they weren't using anymore, and we would come and get them and try to fix them up. They also donated a lot of money. My mom and I would take the money and go Christmas shopping for toys, clothes, and appliances. All of them don't come to the party, but they all get something. Each person would write a list of what they wanted, and we would try to get some things for each of them from their own lists. On our computer, we post all their lists. Some of them go to day programs, some live in group or adult homes, so their families or the staff make sure they get their lists in to us in time.

The first year, I thought we'd just have a Christmas party and that would be it. I expected that maybe twenty or fifty people would come and dance and eat and leave. When 300 people came, I said, "Wow! I can't believe I made all this happen." Then we expanded the project beyond just Christmas. Last year I planned an Easter egg hunt and we filled 597 plastic eggs with money, candy, and toys. I went out and asked for help from everyone, and everything was donated. We even had music by a local DJ who volunteered his time.

It's a lot of work. Not only do I solicit donations and do public relations for the parties, but I recruit volunteers to make decorations and wrap gifts, do some of the shopping, coordinate party events, and I get someone to volunteer to be Santa Claus. I pick up and deliver gifts with my father. Around the holidays especially, I spend a couple of hours every day and eight to ten hours on the weekends. Others help a lot too. Free food gets donated for the Christmas party, and volunteers come to serve and clean up.

The hardest part, though, is not the work, but not being able to buy more than one gift per person, and not being able to reach everyone who could use a gift. Resources are just too limited in our small rural community.

After three years, the recipients now come from not just my mom's caseload and the other seven case managers in her office, but from all ten counties in the area. And though it began with just the mentally handicapped, later I included those with mental illnesses and physical disabilities too. We include people from age 4 to senior citizens.

The first year we gave out 300 gifts. This year we expect to distribute more than 450 gifts. After the Easter egg hunt, I wrote to the newspaper and asked members of the community if they had any passes or season tickets to local amusement parks or sports teams that they would share. A lot of people responded with tickets, and I made arrangements so my special friends could go places. It was really successful. The local radio station has given tickets out too. In one case, some of the young women members of a group home wanted to go on a vacation, but didn't have much money, so I raised some money so they could go and have fun. I'm also trying to raise money for a van that would be used for the youth ministry as well as for taking my disabled friends on trips or to go shopping or to the movies. Last Christmas, I took some of *my* gifts from under the tree in my house and I gave them to some of my disabled friends. I wanted them to feel good and have some nice things too.

Some kids in my school won't talk to the mentally disabled because they're different. But everybody's different—we're all unique. I've really gotten to know these people not only as unique people but as friends.

My advice to other young people is to start small. If you start a project too large to begin with, it builds up and you get stressed.

The parties themselves are wonderful to experience. From the deaf person dancing happily to music, to the people in wheelchairs whose friends push them laughing around the dance floor, it is all so satisfying to see. I learned that it doesn't so much matter what a gift is or how much it costs, but that it comes from someone who cares. The best part is to see people smile and come to me and say, again and again, "Tyrell, thank you, I'm so happy."

Yanick Dalhouse

CHAPTER 14

Yanick Dalhouse:

Empty Bowls, Full Hearts

Born into an African-American family in the South, Yanick Dalhouse found herself somewhat of an outsider when the family moved to Moorhead, Minnesota. She managed to turn her "differentness" into an asset as she presided over a project to sensitize her community to the problems of hunger. Hunger certainly knows nothing about state lines or racial boundaries.

Yanick's Empty Bowls Project provided thousands of dollars to food pantries that serve thousands of hungry people each year. What's more, many individuals in her community became aware for the very first time of how many of their own members don't have enough to eat. Once people are aware, they find it much harder to turn away from those in need. Yanick can take pride in her role in bringing about some of that change.

Don't laugh, but my very first experience in community service wasn't a very pleasant one. It happened when I was 6 years old. My parents quite often donated clothing to different organizations like Boys' Shelter and places like that, and I resisted giving away any of my clothing. In fact, my parents tried to make their point by taking pictures of me wearing clothing that was too small. Children often don't want to part with anything, so I tried my hardest to keep it all, but ended having to give some of it away.

Slowly but surely, through that experience, and also because I'd help my parents serve food at the Salvation Army, I became aware of the issues of homelessness and hunger that we face in our society.

Both my parents are professors, so I had the privilege of growing up in a comfortable home. I grew up, actually, in a unique way, because I was born and raised in the South, in Jackson, Mississippi. And I lived there until I was 8 and in the third grade. Then we moved all the way from the Deep South to Moorhead, Minnesota, where my parents had gotten teaching jobs at Moorhead State University. With that move, I experienced a culture shock like no other. It was a very interesting experience, a major transition.

When I lived in the South, and I have to be very honest, I was quite ignorant. And I think a lot of people fall into that trap. In the South, I associated poverty with African-Americans, because that's what I saw. Even though I was African-American myself! Most of the people that I was helping were black, 95 percent of them. So when I moved up here, it was a much smaller community, and the population was Caucasian. Back in Jackson, because my parents were very educated, most of the Caucasians in the area we lived in were all very well-off. When I got here, I just assumed everyone was middle to upperclass.

Through our church—we're Episcopalian—we began helping out at homeless shelters in Moorhead, and it came as a surprise to me to see white people there. "Oh," I said to myself, "I didn't realize that Caucasian-Americans could be needy as well!" At that point

I did not see one African-American. Here there's a large migrant population, so there were a lot of Hispanics, but I didn't see any African-Americans. It was the same at school and everywhere else.

I got involved in service learning when it was just starting in Minnesota. When I was a junior in high school, I got selected by a teacher to be a student teacher in a trial classroom for service learning for ninth graders. I was also playing basketball at the time, and the teacher in charge of this new program happened to be a basketball coach who I became friends with.

The reason I chose to be so active in service activities was that I got more personal satisfaction out of helping others than I did out of just hanging around. I mean, I enjoyed spending time with friends, but I'm one of those people who thinks there's always something else that could be done.

Also, because my dad is from Jamaica and came into the United States and tried to be successful as a foreigner, and my mom grew up in Kentucky, they've always pretty much ingrained in me that you have to work very hard, especially as a minority. And that's true. I guess they've always said "Push yourself," and "You always have to be thankful for what you have because if you look back to the past, where we've come from. . . ."

That experimental class went wonderfully. I got a chance to interact with students, and we put together projects to educate others. Our projects had to be connected with curriculum and with giving back to the community.

After that, I got a chance to go to the National Service Learning Conference, and that's where I met the coordinator for the North Dakota State University Cass County Extension Office, DeAnn Johnson. She had gotten this grant to put together a youth service group, and it was also at this conference I learned about a small project that had been put on, the Empty Bowls Project. DeAnn asked me if I wanted to be part of a service group, and I was more than willing.

We started to form this new group toward the end of the school year. We deliberated over a name forever. We decided on STARS, which is Students Taking Action Responding with Service. We tried to figure out what service projects we could do. I got announced as the president because I had gotten this idea for the Empty Bowls Project. They said, "Well, since you have the idea, you should be the president."

We wanted to do something big. If there is one cause that I really believe in, besides maybe cancer and AIDS, it's hunger and homelessness. More than 13,000 people seek help from the Fargo-Moorhead Food Pantry in a single year. This Empty Bowls Project had been done in another place, but on a much smaller scale. It's all about getting members of the community to make ceramic bowls to sensitize people about the problems of hunger.

A number of adults told us we couldn't do it. In Fargo-Moorhead, hunger is not as apparent as in, say, Chicago. We kept being told we wouldn't be able to raise much money in this community. Imagine a group of kids trying to accomplish this huge project! These negative people were those we went to and asked for funding to get the group going, to buy us T-shirts to be able to promote ourselves as an organization. They said, "You won't make it." We heard a lot of, "Well, maybe we'll give a few dollars, but we really want to see you guys get started first." One or two companies gave us a chance. Then, of course, after the fact, a lot of people ended up helping.

It was quite a challenge to figure out how we were going to incorporate the Empty Bowls Project into the schools to meet the grant's requirements. I went to talk to the superintendent of schools from Moorhead, and we approached teachers for help. We went to all the art teachers and the community art center in Fargo and asked if they would help us by having people make and donate ceramic bowls. We asked the three colleges in the area to make bowls for us and donate them, which they did.

We put together packets for kindergarten through sixth grade that included exercises, information for teachers on teaching students about homelessness and hunger, crossword puzzles, things to read, and games to play. One of the STARS members drew a picture of a girl looking down into an empty bowl, and then we gave that to all the grocery stores and had a coloring contest. We gave away prizes for that at the Empty Bowls event itself. Then we had students of all ages, from kindergarten through college, making ceramic bowls and told them to come and try to find their bowl at the Empty Bowls banquet. The STARS group even learned how to make the bowls ourselves.

More than 2,000 students, area artists, teachers, and community leaders were involved. Because the event grew so huge, with so many people calling out of the blue asking how they could help, we realized we had to have some sort of big day when we would serve soup in the bowls everyone had been making. Eventually, this all led up to a single big afternoon event that would be held at the North Dakota State University Sports Arena in Fargo.

Home-ec classes and other people came from all over to make bread and soup. The event itself was open to the general public. The main purpose was to have people buy the bowls. And the bowls were actually served with the soup that was made by students and restaurants in the area. To get the bread and soup, you had to purchase a bowl, which kept the homeless themselves from coming because they may not have been able to afford that.

The planning for the big event took a lot of time. I wanted to play basketball too. This was the summertime, and I thought, "Why am I sitting and slaving over this, trying to figure out how to do this?!" My coach was pressuring me to practice all the time, and I wanted to play in college a year later. I'm not tall, but I played point guard and was really fast. I did have to sacrifice going to additional basketball camps after one session. I felt like this was my senior year and I have a chance at least to do *something*.

When we first got turned down by everyone, we thought this was just a bad project, that maybe we should try and look at some other things. I think it helped that I was older and I was able to share my experiences with the group. Also, since I was the only African-American in our group, and a lot of kids had never related to or been very close to African-Americans, when I told them about the satisfaction I got out of helping people, I felt like I somehow had more credibility with them. A lot of them later said that if it hadn't been for me always pushing, they probably wouldn't have done it. I kept telling them what a gratifying experience it would be if we were able to pull this off despite what other people believed.

We had to have the fire inside of us in order to get everybody else out there motivated. That was why it became so hard. We were okay, but we had to go out and keep pushing the people that were saying, "I don't know if this is going to work." It was like a brushfire. It kind of started out slow, and what really got this blazing was that the press caught on. In fact, I recently decided to major in broadcast journalism. I think you can make such an impact on people's lives that way.

All along the way, to comply with the grant, we had to write out everything, from our plan of action to how we were going to carry it out. We invited the Fargo mayor to the main event, and he came and said a few things about how proud he was of us. We had ninth graders who wrote poems about how they felt after users of the Food Pantry came and talked to them about their experiences. The STARS group read more than 100 poems and we chose the five best, and the authors came and read them at the event and got prizes.

The work and planning for the event lasted a span of about four months altogether. I ended up getting in a car accident after school started, just when I was backing off a little from my involvement so I could spend time on basketball, and that ended my basketball career. After that, I completely devoted all my attention to Empty Bowls. We ended up doing five or six things we hadn't planned on, just because I was able to submerge myself in the project. And I *wanted* to.

The main part of the event, where people could choose bowls and eat soup, lasted about an hour and a half. Then two days later the members of STARS met and tallied the money, and that's when we realized we'd made almost $10,000. Our goal originally was to raise only $2,000. We were excited by how much we were able to donate to the Fargo-Moorhead Food Pantry and to the Great Plains Food Bank.

What I would have done just a little bit differently was to try to get more of the people we were directly affecting involved, such as taking volunteers to help make soup and to help serve the soup. A lot of people said afterward, "It would have been nice if you had been able to have some of the people receiving the services there to say thank you." And that's not always easy to do. Sometimes they won't necessarily want to do that.

The best part would have to be the fact that, in life, I can walk away and say that I know I made a difference in at least one person's life. I touched someone else. I feel like I gave something that no amount of money could give. And they gave me something. You can't buy the feelings that I got—being able to give the money to the people who I knew needed it the most and being able to work very hard for something I believed in with all my heart. To be able to have the opportunity to do that was just wonderful.

Lo Detrich

CHAPTER 15

Lo Detrich:

Striding Toward a Normal Future

Lo Detrich doesn't have the luxury of taking breathing for granted. Diagnosed with cystic fibrosis when she was a few months old, the energetic teen doesn't waste precious time feeling sorry for herself. Rather, she gives speeches and raises money so researchers can find a cure for what threatens her life and the lives of 30,000 other young people across the United States. Her project is called Great Strides, and indeed, doctors have made a lot of progress in recent years, offering hope to Lo, her family, and so many others.

It would be easy for a young girl with the number-one genetic killing disease among children and young adults to sit back and wait for someone else to take action. After all, Lo says she only breathes "about half of what you breathe," and describes her illness as like "a really bad case of asthma," except that it damages the pancreas and several other organs too. In order to ensure that the food she eats doesn't go right through her, she takes fifty to sixty pills every single day, including some before every meal and snack.

With all that, Lo personally raised $50,000, and the Great Strides walk she headed raised $100,000 in Tulsa, Oklahoma, alone. Seems like an understatement to say, as Lo does, "We're not big whiners in my family."

Instead of just complaining and having a miserable life because of my disease, and rather than saying, "This just absolutely stinks," I decided to turn it into something more positive by working toward a cure instead of simply heading toward death. I learned that attitude from my family. I've been raised to take something like this and put it into the positive. My parents have been volunteering for cystic fibrosis since I was diagnosed with the disease at 3 months. It's not that we *never* complain, because we're not perfect. But we don't like complaining. We'd rather do something to change the situation.

I was in third grade when I began my own community service. I was sitting in my doctor's office when I noticed a brochure about an event that was coming up for the very first time. Called Great Strides, it was intended to raise money for cystic fibrosis research. Participants walk around the Tulsa Zoo after going house to house, friend to friend, neighbor to neighbor, getting sponsors to pledge a flat donation of money. It was something I could do without having to get my mom's help. That appealed to me.

The first year I participated, I raised around $600. It was a lot of hard work. Ever since then, I've kept on raising more and more.

Every year my enthusiasm and my interest have gone up more too. Finally, two years ago they asked me to be chairperson of the event.

At first, this was a pretty new event, so we were still learning how to do things, how to get people involved. As chairperson, you're in charge and responsible for the whole event. How big or how small you make it is in your hands. You are the one who's going to get people to participate, and you do that by making sure the brochures get distributed and by going out and making speeches at different schools.

Giving speeches wasn't hard for me, since I've been giving speeches since I was really little. I've always been an ambassador, a spokesperson, for cystic fibrosis. When you're trying to get a huge company to donate thousands upon thousands of dollars to something, they're going to want to see someone with the illness. This was even before Great Strides. I think it's turned me into quite a little talker!

My parents were thrilled with my involvement. They thought it was a great idea, and they were behind me 100 percent. They said, "We're here if you need our help."

My friends started raising money too. In fourth grade, I went around and got our school directory and called all my friends' parents and asked them to donate. And then, I just said, "Guys, we're going to the zoo, so why don't you ask *your* friends and *your* parents to help?"

But really, with the friends I have in this community, it doesn't take much to get them motivated. If there's something going on, it's "Hey, let's do it." We absolutely love Great Strides, and we look forward to this event every year because it's so much fun.

Actually, all of my friends' parents and my parents' friends, as well as a lot of local businesses, got involved with cystic fibrosis shortly after I was diagnosed. They took it upon themselves. I have a lot of really great friends who have always supported me in everything I've done. And that is one of my motivations to keep on going day to day. They and my parents and God are my main motivators.

With me being the chairperson the last couple of years, my mom and I took the walk to a higher level. What I mean is that we've gotten not only my school involved, we've turned it into a major kids' event around Tulsa. We've gotten lots of schools around our community involved.

Most of the kids who went to school with me last year made the transition to high school with me too. We've had a lot of fun staying involved with this every year. We've had meetings with about twenty to thirty kids who are the true leaders, who are always there at the Walk. We had around 300 to 400 kids participating last year. And Tulsa is not that big. That many kids on a Saturday morning was really, really awesome.

Though it takes place on one day, we really have to work at it all through the year. In about February, my mom starts calling schools to ask if I can come speak to them. Even though the speeches take a toll on me, I really have a blast doing it. It's a great way to bring the schools together and to show the community how well our teenagers are doing and trying to make a difference in the world. We're highlighting positive attitudes instead of negative ones, for a change!

The money goes to the Cystic Fibrosis Foundation in Washington, D.C. I'm really proud that 91 cents of every dollar they spend goes straight to the research clinics. They're one of the top foundations that way. I feel like the researchers are really using the money well, because they come out with so much medicine, and they've come a long, long way toward producing a cure. I hope and I think they're getting closer every single day.

My mom pretty much did the planning and organizing part. I mainly spoke at schools to get kids excited, wrote letters, and then made what seemed like a million phone calls asking for donations.

Last year I personally raised $50,000. That's not just from neighbors! It mostly came through my parents' friends and this whole network of friends asking friends, all individual donors. I spend a lot of time on the phone. Our phone bill goes way up around April and May. I write letters to all my dad's and mom's friends, and even the people my dad went to high school with. I keep them updated on how I'm doing every year, and every year, they donate.

I get sick a *lot*. I have to do two or three hours of medical stuff a day, well or sick, such as physical therapy, breathing treatments, trying to keep myself going. I'm often hospitalized. It takes a lot of time. I'd much rather be running or playing sports, but I have found that really leaning on my faith has helped me so much. We're getting real involved in our church, and I love youth group. I'm a real social person, so I find time. If there's no time, I'll still find time. I hardly ever watch television, it just really doesn't appeal to me.

I spend so much time collecting money for those distant researchers because someday I would like not to keep getting sick. Hopefully, when I'm older, I won't have to do all this stuff, and I'll have a longer life expectancy, and the way to make that happen is by raising money. When I was born, I wasn't expected to live past 25, and now I'm expected to live till 30. So I decided that I'm not going to let people do that *for* me. I'm going to take that into my hands, and I'm going to help *them* when they want to help me.

Raising this money really motivates me, and when I see the outcome, it's amazing. It's helping people all over the world. And not only is it just helping cystic fibrosis kids, but I think it's changed some people just because they're realizing, no matter what your problem is, the best way to fix it is by trying to make something positive come out of it. Taking what you have and turning it around.

One thing I learned from this project is never to give up. If you always look on the bright side (and make a few dozen more phone calls!), you can reach your goals. One of the most memorable times was when I made a speech to everyone who came to the Great Strides Walk, which was hundreds of people. People were cheering for me, and I saw tears in their eyes.

I do other community work too. When I go with my school to the homeless shelter and help them out, hand out clothes and such, when you show that you're caring, and especially for the kids, it brings about a smile and a happy look in their eyes. And that is one person who had not been reached if it weren't for you. And that might save someone's life.

My advice to other kids is that you're going to get so much more out of seeing someone's life change, or someone just smiling because you did something for them, than watching television or sitting at home. The way I think about it is that when you change someone's life, that's amazing in and of itself.

I've been thinking a lot about my future lately. I would love to be a motivational speaker. I love to teach. And of course, I want to be a mom.

We really need to appreciate what we have, and that will drive us to want to help someone else. Even with the problems I have, I'm still so very blessed.

CHAPTER 16

Marcus Houston:

Football Star Says "Just Say Know"

Thomas Jefferson High School student Marcus Houston is what you might call a football hero. He was selected to the All-Colorado Football Team, named as a USA Today *and* Parade *All-American, and he was chosen by* SuperPrep *magazine as the number-one running back in the country. Not one to brag, Marcus instead uses his high visibility to help his Denver community. With his Just Say Know program, he impresses upon middle-schoolers how important an education is and what it means to be truly successful. He helps them find their passion, and that can make all the difference in a life.*

Marcus Houston

Ever since elementary school, I've been active in my church and on the student council, helping out with canned food and clothing drives. Then, in the middle of my junior year of high school, I started my own program, which I call Just Say Know. I'll tell you why I believe it's so necessary.

On my football team, I learned that a lot of incoming freshman were becoming ineligible due to poor grades or conduct problems or both. I always had older brothers who were a positive influence in my life, so I felt like it was my turn to take responsibility to tell these students what was important. And instead of focusing on incoming freshmen, when it was almost too late, I took it one step farther and decided to start speaking to eighth graders at the middle-school level. I didn't aim my talks only at football players though. I figured that what I had to say would be useful in many aspects of the lives of these students.

I have a passionate approach toward everything I do, whether it's football, school, or student council. I believe that when these eighth-graders find their passion, it's going to have a big impact on how they live their lives. That's how the idea for my essay contest came into play. I can't sit someone down and say, "You look like you'll be a doctor," but what I can do is help motivate students who previously didn't feel that school was important and encourage them to put their own goals on paper, to figure out their own priorities.

I started with a nearby public middle school. I wrote up a proposal, letting the administration know I'd like to put on a forty-five-minute presentation in one classroom. After I did this, I got a lot of positive feedback from the teacher and the administration and the class itself. Then a couple of other teachers called and asked me to put on my Just Say Know program, and I did. It's really grown since then. Now it's the principals and the teachers who call and ask me to do my presentation at their school.

After my talk, I present my essay contest. I have students write about how they view themselves as successful and what they're doing to *be* successful. I believe it's very important to be able to look inside yourself. I don't want the essay to be perceived by the students as just another homework assignment. I want them to really take this to heart. I began by raising $50 by shoveling walks, so I could offer the winner of the essay contest a $50 scholarship. In addition, if 75 percent of the class or more turn in essays, then I sponsor a pizza party for the class.

The students won't look up to just "any old person." The teachers will normally introduce me and tell something about my reputation playing football. Football is pretty popular, so my presentation includes a five- or ten-minute film of highlights from my football career. It has some of the plays from the season. That gets the students excited and pumped up. Some of the girls find that even more exciting than some of the guys do. Often middle-school students will already know which high school they'll be going to, so I work that knowledge into the part of my talk about football teams. I personalize it that way. Then I go on to talk about image, schoolwork, how you have to be dedicated, how school is important, and what to expect of yourself.

The contest only lasts for two weeks after I give my presentation. I read all the essays myself (they're just one page). Along with the essays, the students have to get a letter of recommendation from a teacher, friend, relative, or parent. I choose the winners myself. Then we have the pizza party. Some classes have had 100 percent of the students turning in essays.

I've done the program in auditoriums a couple of times, but I try to keep it to groups of about fifty. Sometimes I do two or three separate talks at one school. Altogether, I've presented Just Say Know to more than 800 middle school students. I've also spoken about my program to a number of professional adult groups that have invited me.

I have a great support system. My parents have always been there for me, but I am also blessed to have two brothers and a sis-

Marcus Houston has much to tell the students he addresses.

ter who help define my success. A lot of my confidence in doing this project comes from the preparation I do. The first time I gave my presentation, I was a little nervous because I wasn't sure how everybody would react. Right afterward, one of the girls came up to me and said with a smile on her face, "You did a great job. This is the first time we've had a speaker and nobody fell asleep." That helped me feel as though I'd done a good job.

Besides the money I make shoveling snow, some people have given me donations to help pay for the scholarships and the pizza parties. I also keep in the back of my mind that "where there's a will, there's a way," which is something that my mom taught me a long time ago. So whenever principals call me and want me to schedule a presentation, I look at my pockets and, if they're empty, I go ahead and schedule it anyway. I just know that somehow the funding will come through. Although I haven't actively solicited funds on a large scale, I've talked about Just Say Know to various people I meet, and I get enough donations that way. And I'm hoping this becomes a national program.

It's a very interactive program. I get a lot of feedback from the audience. They ask me if I want to go to the NFL. I tell them I'd love to, but I'm not planning on it, that I'm planning to get an education. A lot of times, kids see things on television that make them think it's easier to get to be a sports professional than to get their degree, so I try to explain the reality of that to them.

I brought fourteen students to our Homecoming football game: two essay winners and twelve others from various categories that I awarded certificates to, for such things as citizenship. I rented a stretch limousine to take them to the game. They brought posters saying, "Just Say Know." There was a lot of pressure on me to have a great game. I thought everybody was expecting it to look like a highlight film, but I scored on the first play of the game from about sixty yards out. So they had a great time. And that evening, I was crowned Homecoming King. That was just a good day in general.

I haven't talked to an audience yet that hasn't been captivated. They participate fully. They ask me questions about high school in general, peer pressure, what they're going to encounter. It's difficult for some middle school students to find themselves standing out by doing well in school. It's not seen as cool. I try to counteract that. I like to tell them, "Sometimes success comes down to whether you reach for the opportunities or reach for the excuses." Judging from the feedback I've gotten, I feel like I'm really making a difference.

CHAPTER 17

Ariane Wilson:

Helping a Friend Helps a Whole Community

Ariane Wilson is a motivated self-starter who works persistently to achieve her goals, asks for help when she needs it, yet often prefers to work independently. So when a daughter of a Spanish-speaking friend of the family found herself in need of free or inexpensive clinic services, Ariane went all out to research, write, translate into Spanish, and print a brochure for her. Of course, Ariane soon realized this information would be useful for many other Hispanics in the diverse communities of Northern California's San Mateo and Santa Clara Counties. She has since distributed some 3,000 copies of "Guía Médica: Una Referencia para Servicios Médicos, gratis o economicos" throughout her four-city, two-county area.

Ariane Wilson

Like many community-service projects, this one took more time than expected. But the rewards were so much greater than expected too. How can the frustration of trying to lay out a brochure by hand be compared to the satisfaction of seeing a total stranger pick up her brochure at a clinic and carefully read it?

I first began volunteering as a member of the Girl Scouts, an organization that stresses community service. I can't even recall the first time I did something for others. It was probably when I was a Daisy Scout in kindergarten and made cookies for residents of a local nursing home.

Through the years, I also did a lot of environmental activities, both through the Scouts and through environmental organizations. I've cleaned beaches, rivers, creeks, and national and state parks, cleared exotic plant species from public lands, planted and tended seedlings in the foothills, staffed booths on Earth Day, and recycled at school and camp. I've collected food, clothes, books, and money for homeless organizations.

Two of the Scout projects I found the most fun were making up toys as part of To Kids From Kids, and acting in Whodunits on board trains during trips. I did the Whodunit performances as a member of Act Out Speak Up, an acting group that deals with problem issues for teens. In the To Kids From Kids project, we made stuffed animals and later packaged the toys and made gift bags for needy children. I loved that project. We had such a good time, not just making the stuffed animals, but going up to a church in San Mateo to package the gift bags. We got little tags, each listing a child's name and age, and then we'd go around to the piles of gifts that people had brought to be packaged. I remember thinking, "I

Ariane Wilson's efforts have made clinics accessible to many people.

really hope he likes this," and "It's going to be so great when she gets this." It was like I knew who the kids were, how old they were, what they might like. It added a human dimension to the project.

When I got to be a Cadette Girl Scout, I was working toward a Silver Award. For my Silver Project, I taught a series of hands-on science classes to girls: physics, astronomy, geology, and chemistry. I kept telling the girls in my classes, "Science is cool. It's not just for boys. Girls can do anything they want to."

There has not been a year since kindergarten when I haven't been involved in community and school service projects at least once a month, and it was usually more than once a week plus most of my summers. The "Guía Médica" brochure, however, was the most time consuming and the most rewarding of all the projects I've done, and looks like it will be the most long-term.

This is how "Guía Médica" came about. Friends of mine from El Salvador and from Mexico mentioned that they needed help finding affordable health care in a clinic where Spanish is spoken. Since I've taken Spanish in school and can speak it fairly well, I realized I could help them. One of my friends had a pregnant daughter who was particularly interested in finding out about prenatal services, so I started calling local clinics and hospitals. What I found out was absolutely amazing. There are so many programs, some of them free and the rest low-cost on a sliding scale. They're offered in Spanish, which is the incredible thing.

I eventually went and visited the clinics and other organizations, and I asked them, "Do you have a brochure that details your services for Hispanics?" They'd say, "Oh well, we have a sheet, but it's in English," or they'd say "We have a brochure for our own clinic, but nothing for the county."

There was nothing out there that had everything that was needed. Even though good health care and good prenatal care are known to make a big difference in how kids turn out, and there is a lot of help available to immigrants in my area, the unfortunate thing is that many of them don't know what's out there, how it can help them, and how to access it.

After I wrote up the information and translated it into Spanish, I thought, "Why should I just give this to just a few friends? Why not help a whole bunch of people?"

That's when the project got really complicated. The really time-consuming part was translating it. I'm not a native Spanish speaker. A lot of the idiomatic expressions are very difficult. I wrote up a preliminary copy and, at the time, my Spanish teacher actually lived across the street from me, so I'd go over there at night and ask her to look at it. She was such a help. I also got help from family friends who would read it and say what was right and what was wrong. "You need to say this, this is kind of awkward," that sort of thing. I could not have done it on my own!

Another time-consuming thing was the layout. I'm not high-tech, so had to do it by hand, cutting and pasting computer text and titles into panels. The finished brochure is 11 by 17 inches [27.9 by 43.2 centimeters], folded into thirds, with a graphic on the front panel, a map on the back two panels, and the clinic information inside. The map took forever! I tried to find a map that I could borrow, but that didn't turn out, so I had to do the lettering by hand. I put a number on each service that matched a number on the map. And I included some bus information. I also included 800 numbers and programs that provide groceries, hot meals, shelter, clothes, money for rent and bills and even cars.

I ended up making copies myself at a local copy shop, then my sister and I folded them. First thing, I gave it to the family friend who needed it. Then I thought about where they'd be most useful. Obviously, I put them in all the clinics, since people might pick them up there and take them to someone else, or maybe the clinic they picked it up at turned out not to be the closest one to them. I made and distributed, total, probably 3,000 copies.

I put them in libraries, and in the Boys and Girls Clubs, because parents come in there to pick up their kids. I also put them in community centers and other places where there's a lot of traffic. I had to get help for the distribution, since I didn't drive. I had to recruit drivers who would wait while I dropped off brochures. I even gave some to my friend, the one whose daughter we did it for, to distribute on buses! And she gave them all out and asked for more. She told me how meaningful it is to provide this information to a mother with a sick child who is new to the area and speaks only Spanish.

This is not the kind of project that appeals to very many kids in my high school, where the party scene is pretty time-consuming. My particular group of friends wasn't into wild parties, but I never really discussed this project with them. When I won a Rotary Club scholarship and the president read off my achievements, one school friend said, "I had no idea you did any of this!"

I learned that there is such a need out there. In fact, I'm working on another guide, this time in English, because so many people have asked me for one. I'm starting a non-profit corporation for "Guía Médica," so I can expand into other communities and even do a Web site in Spanish. I'm really interested in public health as a career, and I'm totally committed to going into it. I plan to earn both an M.D. and a Ph.D.

If I have any advice for teens, I would say that it pays to be creative when thinking of ways to help your community. You don't have to join someone else's project if you don't find your own talents and interests best used that way. You can start something on your own. The more you love what you're doing, and the better you are at it, the more valuable your contribution can be. I like to work with others, but I love doing my own projects—my own ideas, my own implementation, my own creative focus, my own look at the Big Picture of how what I'm doing helps society in general.

There were lots of "best parts" to this project. Seeing the look on the face of our friend when I handed her "Guía Médica," and she said, "Muchísimas gracias! Lo necessité tanto!" Going back to the clinics and having the nurse say, "Oh, we're out of 'Guía Médica,' we need some more." Seeing people pick up the brochure at places I'd left them and wanting to go speak to them. I almost said something to a woman who picked one up at a clinic, but I didn't. I just watched her read it. That was really cool.

Todd Wheeling

CHAPTER 18

Todd Wheeling:

High-Tech Help for Rural Students

Tenth-grader Todd Wheeling didn't think it was fair that the 500 students in his rural Gaylesville, Alabama, school had much less access to computers than students in larger schools. His peers in kindergarten through twelfth grade had no way to learn to type, much less to learn those skills crucial to a computerized world. So Todd decided to raise funds for computers for his school. But, going beyond the obvious, he also built the computers himself from components, making his appeal to the community much more effective and saving the school a lot of money. When he graduated, Todd left behind a fully equipped computer lab, giving his hometown school a high-tech entry into the twenty-first century.

I joined the school newspaper staff in the ninth grade. In those days, we only had one or two old, obsolete computers in a corner of the room where we put the newspaper together. All told, there were about four other computers in the school, and they were way out of date. Even those were in the administrative offices, not necessarily available for students to learn on.

In the beginning of the tenth grade, I became the editor of the school paper and kept that position until I graduated. I saw an immediate need for new computers, as far as the newspaper staff was concerned. But moreover, just in general, what really bothered me was that typing was no longer taught in my school. You would have had to go to a vocational school to take a typing course. The lack of teaching typing skills really disturbed me, because everybody needs typing these days.

The newspaper advisor and I had several conversations about how we could raise money to buy a few computers for a combined newspaper lab and computer lab that would be accessible to the rest of the school. I suggested maybe we could raise money to build them, rather than to buy them. I already had some experience building computers at a local manufacturing plant. I had worked summers doing computer repair work there. And at that point I had just built a computer for myself. In fact, I'm planning to make computer science and electrical engineering my career, so I've always had this sort of interest. It was natural to think of how to combine my interests and skills with making a real difference in my own school.

I also thought that if we were actually building computers, it might be easier to raise the money. It might be more appealing to donors to help us out. Along the same lines, we came up with the idea that we could apply to the Board of Education for matching funds. At the time, the reason there were no computers in the school was that there was no budget for them. Now it's different and there's a technology budget, but that wasn't the case just a couple of years ago. They were more likely to match our funds if we were going to build the computers, not just buy them.

We organized quite a few projects to begin raising the money we needed for the computer components. It was the newspaper staff and the members of student government—I was involved in that too—who did almost all the work. We had spaghetti dinners before football games, including the Homecoming game, that we charged for. That brought in a lot of money. We had a big all-day event for school alumni on a Saturday. We called it "Coming Home." We explained our project to everyone and got donations on a person-by-person basis. We sold candy as one of the ongoing fund-raisers, as well as athletic T-shirts, pens, pencils, and stickers.

We didn't have a specific amount of money as a goal. We planned to keep raising funds until May, the end of the school year, then to ask for matching money from the Board of Education. Then we'd build what we could, and then we'd start over again the following year.

Once we had some money, including the matching funds from the Board of Education, and some donations from three area mills, I started shopping for good prices. I called around to a couple of companies I'd had past experience with and talked to some sales representatives. I chose one company, and we stuck with them through the rest of the project.

Over the summer, over the course of several evenings after work, I built the computers and installed the software. After I completed a couple myself, I showed some students from the newspaper staff how to do it. It's not too complicated, as long as you have the right parts on hand—unless you run into problems. I also ordered some networking equipment and cable and networked the computers. We bought a scanner too. I figure we saved about a third of the price on the computers by building them instead of buying them already put together.

When I was in the eleventh grade, we had built about eight or nine computers, and our computer lab was looking pretty nice. As far as the newspaper was concerned, we were a whole lot better off than we had been before, but one thing we thought it would be nice to have was a sturdy printer that could print on tabloid-size paper. The tabloid-size printers were very expensive, so I figured I could give a shot at talking to some companies. I thought at the most we might get a good discount. One of the companies I talked to was Hewlett Packard. I found out they had an ongoing philanthropy program with the schools, and it turned out that their Southern section felt they had been neglecting the high schools. Anyway, I was told to write up a good proposal, which I did, and they donated a really expensive printer to us. We were thrilled.

We were also able to get a lot of money from the County Commissioner's office. I spoke to one of the commissioners, and the newspaper advisor spoke to another one. In the end, we were able to build more than fifteen computers.

I had three really good friends on the newspaper staff who helped the most. We all tried to get the other staffers and student government members motivated and working. There was frustration. Sometimes people would say they'd show up somewhere and they wouldn't. A lot of them were interested so long as the activities were during school when they could possibly get out of class, when it was just something to do. But after school and on Saturdays, that's when it was frustrating to get people to come and help. There were ten or fifteen participants, but only four or five on an ongoing basis.

The best part was seeing the end result, seeing those computers there for students to use. Now students are learning to type, use word-processing programs and spreadsheets, and so on. The newspaper staff is able to produce the whole newspaper by computer, and they're gaining insights into desktop publishing. A few students were more verbal in their thanks than others, but I didn't think much about that part. That's not what I did it for.

However difficult a project is, you take it one step at a time, and everything will probably fall into place. It's definitely worth it.

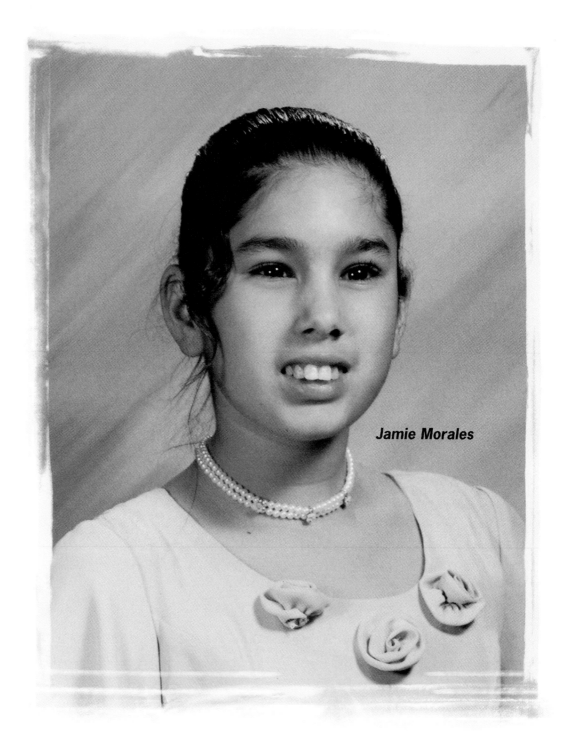

Jamie Morales

CHAPTER 19

Jamie Morales:

Choosing to Save Lives

When Jamie Morales was 5, her godfather died of AIDS. When she was 6, her Uncle Jeff died of the same dread disease. Worst of all, when Jamie was only 7, her mother also died of it. On top of all that, her father is currently living with AIDS.

Amazingly, at only 8 years of age, Jamie was able to begin bouncing back from these tragedies. She became an active volunteer spreading the facts about AIDS—beginning in Wichita, Kansas—so others might avoid going through pain like hers. Her guardian, Sandy Hysom, who has been raising Jamie since her mother died, conducts HIV/AIDS programs as part of her job at the American Red Cross, and what could be more natural than that Jamie would soon want to do programs of her own?

And what could have more impact than listening to someone your own age who really knows what she's talking about?

When I first moved in with Sandy, my guardian, after my mom died, she was doing programs about HIV and AIDS as part of her job as Youth Services Director for the Red Cross. Since I was only 8, I'd go with her rather than stay home with a babysitter. I'd usually sit in the back and color pictures and watch. After listening to her programs so often, I knew them by heart. I thought what Sandy was doing looked really interesting, and I asked her if I could help her out. I started by drawing some of the pictures and diagrams that were part of the programs. Soon I started talking about my mom to the audiences.

At first, Sandy didn't think I should do this, because I was so young and AIDS was such a controversial subject. But she asked my counselor, and the counselor felt it would be good for me to do if it was something I was comfortable doing.

My first program was when I was 8 years old. I spoke at a church group of parents and their kids, about twenty-five people. Then I spoke to a PTA group. Sandy is usually there when I do programs, since I can't drive myself, though occasionally now I'll do them alone. Sometimes I've even gotten my dad to come along and participate in a program. When I was 13, I developed a slide show. The difference between the programs now and when I was 8 is that I've added on a lot. It's longer, about an hour, and there are more statistics compared to when I started.

The biggest group I have spoken to was 700 middle-schoolers in an assembly. By now, I've educated thousands of people with my programs. Wichita State University Media Resource Center, with the sponsorship of the AIDS Fund, made a videotape of my talk so the message can reach even more people. To help a fund-raiser for the AIDS Fund, I made some art work that represented my mom and the fourteen cats we had. The art was transferred to a scarf that sold for $505. Ten more of my scarves are now for sale by an AIDS organization in New York City, Broadway Cares.

My main motivation is that I don't want anyone to learn about the disease the way I did, through hard experiences. My dad is presently living with AIDS, and I talk about what his life is like and all the medicines he has to take. I also focus on the latest information and statistics about HIV and AIDS and how kids can protect themselves.

I do these programs mainly in Wichita, but also all over Kansas. I get called to do programs at schools and churches, rather than having to call them myself to set them up. When I go to a school, one teacher will tell another teacher, and that one will call me and say, "Would you come and do a program?" I speak to middle-school students on up to adults. At each Wichita school I've been to, you have to have your parents sign a permission slip in order to hear me.

I try to even out my absences from school, doing one program in the afternoon of one school day, and another in the morning of another day, so I don't miss too much of anything. It's considered a school-related absence. The talks I do may not "count" for anything in high school, though I know it does look good on a college application. But I never did it for that, and I never even thought it was possible for me to win any awards for this.

A lot of my friends reacted with surprise when I began doing programs. A lot of them knew my mom had died but they didn't know how. I always wanted people to get to know me as me, before I told them about that. All their reactions have been really good. I've never lost any friends because of telling them the truth. Actually, they thought I was brave for speaking openly about this personal subject.

This is also my second year of "official" involvement in a Teens Hope group, which is made up of high school kids who attend a

Jamie Morales has helped educate people about AIDS.

two-day training and who then go to their own schools to educate their peers about AIDS, such as in P.E. classes. I've actually been training members of the group since I was really little. We also speak to sixth-grade science classes.

I try to keep up on all the latest information about AIDS. I especially love going to conferences and learning more about my subject, and then going and doing the programs. Sometimes I'm involved in a conference, such as last year when I got to speak at the National Ryan White Youth Conference in Boston. That's really exciting and absorbing. It's fun to learn about what you're doing.

My big message directed to people my age is, "Choose not to get AIDS." A lot of the time, I do realize they *are* listening to me, because I'm someone their own age they can relate to. Sometimes I get questions from my audiences, and sometimes I don't get any. Actually, the younger kids ask a lot more questions, but I think it hits the older ones, in high school, a lot harder because they know other young people who are doing things that put themselves at risk.

I plan to keep doing these presentations in the future, in my spare time. My first and foremost career will be with animals, though, since I've always loved working with them. I've volunteered at the zoo, working side by side with the zookeepers.

But that's not all I've done. I've volunteered at the Red Cross every summer. I love to perform theater with Music Theater of Wichita. I've been on track, volleyball, and basketball teams. I'm in the marching band. Right now I'm in the very first statewide group of a drum corps color guard.

I'm really lucky. I've gotten to have a lot more opportunities and chances than a lot of people have. I've won awards, and I've gotten to go places and meet new people. But to speak to groups, I've had to grow up a lot faster than most kids. I would trade it all if I could have my family back.

I have a lot of fun with the volunteering. It's a really good inspiration when you know people are listening to you. I've gotten letters from people, teens especially, who've heard me speak. That's really the best part, hearing people tell me I've been such a help to them, or that I've inspired them in some way.

Matt
Nonnemacher

CHAPTER 20

Matt Nonnemacher:

Every Little Bit Helps

When Matt Nonnemacher was only 9 years old, he started a project that made a difference in his life and in the lives of countless others. His plan was to collect a million pennies for the poor. By the time his project was complete eight weeks later, he had managed to gather more than 1.8 million pennies—that's more than $18,000—to be used for the charitable works of the United Way of Greater Hazleton, Pennsylvania. The tremendous interest and support of his community amazed Matt and his family. And Matt learned that one small generous action can lead to a huge chain of positive results.

I had never done any kind of community service project before, but my parents had talked about the poor, so I always knew they were there. When I was 9 and in fourth grade, my teacher gave us a homework assignment to draw our "one wish" in the world. I came home, went up to my room, and thought about what to wish for. I decided to draw a picture showing myself giving money to the poor.

When I showed this picture to my mom and dad, they encouraged me to do something to make this wish come true. So I wrote a letter to our local newspaper asking people to send me ideas on how to help the poor. One person suggested I have a dime drive. I changed it to pennies so kids would think it was more fun to donate and collect them.

My dad took me to the United Way because they help a lot of poor people, and I decided that I would donate the money I collected to them. While I was there, they took a picture of me holding a regular jar of pennies in front of a bank vault. The local newspaper used the picture when they ran a story about how I wanted to collect a million pennies in the next two months—by Make a Difference Day in October.

Then things started happening. About 800 clear mayonnaise jars were donated by a local plastics manufacturing company. We cut out my picture from the newspaper, shrunk it and made copies, and then used that as one of the labels for the jar. My dad made the other label on his word processor. It explained my goal and said, "A Million Ways to Care," which became the name of my project. Some of the mentally challenged clients from a United Way agency put the labels on the jars. A local machine shop cut a slot in all the jar lids so coins could fit through.

We put the jars in each classroom at my school, and at the end of the month, whichever classroom had the most money was given a pizza party. We also put them in businesses and stores, like supermarkets and Wal-Mart. People called us and asked for jars. My father and mother drove me everywhere to put out the jars. Then our principal called other schools, and they wanted to collect too.

My friends were excited about putting pennies in the jars. I put some of my own allowance in too. By the end of the first weekend, when we went around to check on them, we saw that some of the jars were already almost filled to the top.

I spent several hours each week for eight weeks on the project. A lot of groups in our town called us and said they would collect pennies for my project. We had to go to their meetings to pick up the jars before the final date. I went with my dad to some place almost every night to pick up pennies, because these groups wanted to see me in person and talk to me about my goal.

When we collected the jars from places, we would bring them to our cellar. Pennies are very heavy. They weighed our car down! Some people would call us to come pick up pennies and they would have a baggie with only 50 cents in it. But we always went and got them. It was important to us to let everyone feel as though they were helping. And they really were.

Some of the pennies we picked up would be in coffee cans and every kind of container. As we collected them, we put them all in the same two-quart jars so we would know how much we had. We even took the silver money out and separated it on our kitchen table. Some of the groups wanted us to tell them how much they had donated, so we had to figure that out. About $25 worth of pennies would fit in a jar that was filled to the top.

For a few weeks, we stored the pennies in our cellar, and later the drop-off place was in the gym at the Jewish Community Center. The United Way arranged for a flatbed truck and a driver to get the pennies from the center and bring them to the bank on the last day. A long line of volunteers—adults and kids—handed the bags of pennies from one to the other from the gym to the truck. There was a kind of parade to the bank, made up of cars and the flatbed truck and school buses that had pennies in them too. Then the volunteers lined up all over again to move the pennies from the truck into the bank. I rode in a police car and got to blow the siren. The newspaper came too.

We brought the pennies to the bank after the bank was going to be closed, because counting so much money was going to be a big job. The bank arranged to get three extra coin counting machines besides the one they already had. The pennies were on counters and the floor, and all the volunteers and bank employees were helping. It took thirteen hours to count all the pennies!

I would tell other young kids that you can do everything you want to. My goal was to collect a million pennies, and we ended up with almost two million. We put up a Web site (www.pennyboy.org) that explains how to do a penny drive, and now groups all around the world are doing penny drives of their own. It's a wonderful feeling to know that I and my family and friends had something to do with this, and that a lot of poor people will have food and clothing and a place to stay because of my wish.

Appendix A

How to Get Started as a Volunteer

Once you've read these teens' inspiring stories, you'll want to do something to help your community too. To begin making a difference, and to experience those terrific feelings you've been reading about, here is some guidance on how to take the next step.

How to Determine the Best Project for YOU

Jot down your thoughts in answer to the following questions:

1. When you read the newspaper or listen to the radio or watch TV news, what gets you upset and makes you want to change something?

2. Have you noticed something in your community that makes you say, "That's not fair! Somebody should do something." Maybe you could be that somebody.

3. What do you think of as your "community"? Is it your own extended family, or does your feeling of connection extend to your classroom or school? Or do you think of yourself as part of your town, your state, your country, or as a citizen of the whole world? Or perhaps you feel most connected to a group of people who share your interests or are like you in some way, such as those with a similar illness, or others who love reading or sports? Some teens have raised money for cystic fibrosis, some who are recovering from addictions have devoted their

time to helping the addicted, while some who love reading have helped others learn to read, or provided equipment so that those less fortunate could enjoy basketball or some other sport they love.

4. Would you like to learn skills you'll use in school too, and perhaps later in your career, or is your primary desire to fix some societal problem?

5. What skills do you already have? For instance, are you good at theater arts, do you have technical skills, are you a great swimmer, are you comfortable meeting and talking to strangers? Do you work well with younger children? List everything you're good at and like to do. Any of these might open the door to a project idea.

6. Would you prefer a one-time short-term commitment, a project that you can complete in a month or two, or something ongoing and open-ended? How much time do you realistically have to devote to a project?

7. Do you prefer working with friends, family, schoolmates, or strangers, or by yourself?

8. Do you want to be a leader? If so, consider starting a group of your own. Or perhaps you'd rather limit your involvement to being the best possible participant in an existing group (at least until you've gained experience and confidence).

What If You're Shy?

When you read about the range of community-service projects young people often get involved in, a lot of them seem to require public speaking and asking unknown adults for donations or help. So what do you do if you're on the shy side or prefer to work more on your own? Go back to Ariane Wilson's story: She researched and created a brochure in Spanish that directed people to helpful free and low-cost resources in the community. Or consider Molly Vandewater's project: She devoted all her free time to helping animals.

Read through the list of additional award-winning projects in Appendix B. There you'll find a teen who raised puppies to become seeing-eye dogs for the blind, another who sewed cloth "caddies" for use by those in wheelchairs, and yet another who tutored youngsters out of his own home, a one-on-one kind of service that can be easier for some people than dealing with larger groups. Others designed landscaping projects, or babysat during PTA meetings, or provided some kind of computer assistance where needed.

Also, think about the teens whose stories are included in this book. Most of them say they didn't start out speaking comfortably to crowds. They didn't wake up one day and decide it would be fun to knock on a lot of doors or make telephone calls to the heads of local businesses. What happened, rather, was that these activities just evolved naturally over time as part of their passion for their chosen project. And little by little, they grew comfortable speaking up and speaking out. In fact, many of the award-winning teens say that is one of the most important things they learned from their projects: to speak publicly about something they believe in, in order to have an impact on others and make change happen.

Researching the Right Project

Once you've narrowed your interests somewhat, continue to take your time before diving into a project. Find out as much as you can first, so you're more likely to find a good fit. Appendix C contains a list of organizations that use volunteers. You'll also find many Internet sites that list groups and resources that can get you started. Many of these sites have links to additional sites.

Consider the following resources as you go about your search: your teacher, principal, and school counselor; your church or synagogue; civic groups in your community, such as the Elks, Rotary, Kiwanis, and Lions clubs; local arts centers or community theaters; food pantries, shelters for the homeless and battered women; zoos, conservation groups, animal shelters; hospitals, hospices, nursing homes; local libraries; and residential facilities for the disabled or for abused children. Don't forget to see what your local newspaper, television, and radio stations have to say about community needs.

How to Get Help from Others

Publicity is important for many community-service projects. If you're collecting used greeting cards, clothing, food, or books, you have to let the community know what you need and where and how to contribute. If your project needs money to succeed, you have to spread the word as widely as possible.

The way you get publicity is by printing up fliers, sending news releases to newspapers, radio, and TV stations, by writing and mailing letters to friends and friends of friends, by putting up notices and posters, by placing ads, and by announcing your needs on computer bulletin boards. There's lots of information available on the best ways to get publicity, much of it available free on Internet sites devoted to service.

In addition to using publicity in the media to get your project known, you may want to personally contact other individuals and businesses to convince them your project is a worthy one to which to donate money and materials. Plan this part carefully, so you demonstrate that you know what you're doing. If you appear confident, competent, and courteous, not to mention excited about what you're doing, others will more likely want to assist you and contribute to your project. You may want to write letters first, and then follow up by phone.

When you ask to speak to a manager, be as organized about what you're asking for as possible, so as not to waste anyone's time. You may not always hear a "yes" in response to your requests for help, but hearing the "no's" will get easier as you have more practice. Persistence is the key to your project's success—though this doesn't mean pestering the same person over and over, but rather having the energy to keep trying other people until you get what you need and what your project deserves.

Another kind of help you may need is from other would-be volunteers. How do you get friends, schoolmates, and even young people who don't know you at all to give their time and energy to something you're passionate about? If you're doing something you really care about, your enthusiasm will be contagious. Learn to describe your project and the needy people you want to help as though you're telling a story. Share with your friends and schoolmates why this subject has touched you so much, what you hope to accomplish, and why it *must* happen. And then tell them how much fun you're all going to have working together on this, and mean it!

And don't forget to thank everyone who helps you. No matter how busy you are, everyone likes to be appreciated, and people are more likely to keep working hard if their efforts are noticed.

Tips to Keep in Mind as You Begin

1. Be persistent. Even before you can get started working with an existing group, you might have to make several calls. Those who work with volunteers are often overworked themselves. Don't give up before you begin!

2. Flexibility helps. No volunteer service project goes just exactly as you think it will. You may be dealing with a number of other personalities, and you all need to learn to get along. That can take time. So be patient and keep an open mind.

3. Learn all you can. Attend orientation meetings, read any manuals, reports, and newsletters that are available, keep up to date on the facts about your project. If there's training available, take it! Read one or more of the books listed in Appendix E of this book for practical suggestions about the actual carrying-out of various kinds of projects.

4. Be responsible. People are counting on you, both other volunteers and those you're trying to help. Treat your volunteer activities as seriously as you would a paying job.

5. Be realistic. Unless you're the one who started the project, you may have to start at the bottom and do more basic work in order to prove your abilities before you move up. If you stick with any project, you will usually have a chance to take on more interesting tasks as time goes by.

6. Make your age work for you. Even though some adults may not take you seriously at first, they soon will. Your age is an advantage. When Brian Harris wanted to start a pen pal exchange, he managed to get several major television programs to give him a spot. They saw his youth as newsworthy, and those TV appearances contributed greatly to making his project a huge success.

7. Avoid burnout. When obstacles threaten to overwhelm you or halt the progress of your project, stop a moment and take stock. Can you take a break? Are your expectations realistic? Never hesitate to ask for more help or to seek out additional emotional support. Someday, when you look back, all the effort will have been worth it—but if you overwork yourself, you may not reach that point. So get enough rest and relaxation.

Appendix B

200+ *Ideas from Recipients of The Prudential Spirit of Community Award*

What can a young volunteer do? There are literally millions of opportunities to make an important difference in the lives of others. Following are more than 200 specific projects that have actually been carried out over the past several years by young people who have won Prudential Spirit of Community Awards. Perhaps their activities will give you some ideas as to what you can do in your own neighborhood or town to help make life better for someone else.

Raise Money for an Important Cause

Kristen Andersen of Ladue, Missouri, started an annual softball game featuring local celebrities, which has raised more than $100,000 for Alzheimer's Disease research.

Richard Hiatt of Los Alamitos, California, organized a walk-a-thon at a local high school to benefit the Children's Cancer Center at the Long Beach Memorial Medical Center.

Jason Crowe of Newburgh, Indiana, started a newspaper "by kids and for kids" to raise money for the American Cancer Society and to show that kids' voices matter.

Lynnea McElreath of Southern Pines, North Carolina, wrote to celebrities to ask for donations of unwanted items and then auctioned them off to raise money to start a homeless shelter in her community.

Courtland Kerstetter of Camden, Delaware, started a food-vending service at single-A baseball parks to raise money for the Make-A-Wish Foundation.

Dana Walsh of Oceanside, New York, organized a student telephone campaign that raised $3,000 from community members for the Cystic Fibrosis Foundation.

Kelly Kessler of Wantage, New Jersey, raised $1,176 for cancer research by organizing a fund-raising competition among homerooms at her school.

Jared Van Ittersum of Spring Lake, Michigan, raised more than $9,000 for the American Lung Association by collecting pledges and then riding his bicycle across the country.

Randi Schamerhorn of Leesville, Louisiana, helped organize a roller-skating "skate-a-long" for which more than 400 people in her community collected pledges for cystic fibrosis research.

Katie Eller of Tulsa, Oklahoma, set up more than 200 lemonade stands in her town and raised more than $20,000 to purchase toys, playground equipment, cribs, and emergency supplies for a homeless facility.

Jeffrey Lange of Wellesley, Massachusetts, recorded and sold a music CD to raise more than $1,000 for the Massachusetts Breast Cancer Coalition.

Robyn Hyle of Cincinnati, Ohio, hosted annual carnivals in her backyard for local youngsters to raise money for the American Cancer Society.

Jennifer Kraschnewski of Burlington, Wisconsin, raised $1,525 for the Make-A-Wish Foundation by recruiting sponsors for the launching of 950 balloons, which contained slips of paper stating the purpose of the launch and the sponsor's name.

Amy Flavin of Lawton, Michigan, organized a wheelchair basketball game at her school to raise money for a coach who had been severely injured in an auto accident.

Help the Sick

Alexia Abernathy of Cedar Rapids, Iowa, served on the board of a home for AIDS patients, helping to raise operating funds, handling numerous chores, and providing companionship to the residents.

Erin Carney of Baltimore, Maryland, volunteered to provide comfort and companionship to young patients at a local hospital, and **Lindsey Childers** of North Platte, Nebraska, volunteered at her local hospital, organizing patient charts, filing, faxing, and performing other needed tasks.

Matthew Green of Titusville, Florida, created an Internet site offering information and advice for teens who suffer from Crohn's disease.

Brooke Lyons of Woodbridge, Connecticut, started a support and information network for individuals with scoliosis and their families.

Gregory Bonetti of Warwick, Rhode Island, organized a petition drive for increased government funding of cancer research, chaired fund-raisers at his school, and assisted with cancer screenings for senior citizens.

Jennifer Koeppel of Snyder, New York, chaired an AIDS awareness committee at her school that collects money and gifts for people with AIDS.

Kathryn Phillips of Rome, New York, recruited nearly 200 people to sign up with the National Bone Marrow Registry, and raised $4,000 to pay for their blood tests.

Andre Beaulieu of Honolulu, Hawaii, volunteered for the American Red Cross, dispatching ambulances, setting up electrocardiograms, answering telephones, and tracking patients' progress.

Megan Leaf of Bel Air, Maryland, founded a program that assembles and distributes gift bags each month to pediatric patients at Johns Hopkins Children's Center.

James Edwards of Tulsa, Oklahoma, recruited fellow students to serve as "big brothers" or "big sisters" to young children with cancer.

Patricia Williams of Bay St. Louis, Mississippi, organized a Halloween party for young cancer patients.

Aaron Romero of Honolulu, Hawaii, dressed up as a clown and performed magic and clown shows at hospitals and homeless shelters.

Joel Yeaton of Exeter, New Hampshire, created a fund to support spinal-cord research and to buy computers for kids to use while they're in the hospital.

Marc Elliot of Chesterfield, Missouri, started an annual toy sale to raise money for the playroom at St. Louis Children's Hospital.

Kathy Beck of Lamesa, Texas, founded a program that decorates and distributes caps to cancer patients who have lost hair from treatments.

Vicki Prautzsch of Hill City, South Dakota, and **Chris Johnson** of Smyrna, Delaware, volunteered as emergency medical technicians for their local volunteer ambulance services.

Enable the Disabled

Caitlin Janus of Barre, Vermont, organized a horseback-riding program for handicapped children.

Alia Szopa of Manchester, New Hampshire, provided dance instruction to pre-teen girls with developmental disabilities.

Matthew McDaniel of Caldwell, Idaho, helped a group of mentally and physically disabled people enjoy the sport of bowling once a week at a local bowling alley.

Natasha Liebig of Chugiak, Alaska, volunteered to help autistic children overcome the challenges they face in everyday life.

Erin Mitchell of Londonderry, New Hampshire, created a "Girl's Group" that paired girls from her scouting troop with girls who have disabilities and took them on recreational outings.

Sarah Baker of Auburn, Washington, raised three puppies to become seeing-eye dogs for Guide Dogs for the Blind, Inc.

Nicole Armand of Bush, Louisiana, organized a private evening of fun at an amusement park for children with epilepsy.

Elizabeth Cable of Mountain City, Tennessee, sewed cloth "caddies" that can be used by people in wheelchairs to hold personal items.

Noel McDaniel of St. George, Utah, designed and distributed a monthly handout showing sign language for curriculum-based vocabulary words to help students with language disabilities.

Help the Abused and Traumatized

Anne Treat of Fargo, North Dakota, volunteered at a rape and abuse crisis center and organized an annual "Take Back the Night" march to honor survivors of abuse and reclaim the safety of the streets.

Ann Nelson of Jasper, Alabama, conducted a drive to collect food, baby items, and other supplies for a local center for abused women and their children.

Shemilly Briscoe of Pahrump, Nevada, organized a three-hour talent show and a raffle that raised more than $1,000 to support a local domestic crisis-intervention shelter.

Samantha Crow of Topeka, Kansas, collected more than 1,700 books to establish a children's library at a home for battered women.

Brandy Hoskins of New Albany, Indiana, conducted a campaign in her school to educate fellow students about child abuse and to raise money for abuse-prevention efforts.

Angela Budge of Orem, Utah, persuaded a group of high school students to make stuffed animals for fire and rescue squads, who then gave the toys to children displaced by accident, fire, or abuse.

Encourage Other Young People to Volunteer

Lisa Guttentag of Greensboro, North Carolina, founded a teen volunteer group that has worked with community organizations to host parties for homeless children, prepare Thanksgiving meals for needy families, and make teddy bears for children's hospitals.

Lisa-Anne Furgal of Largo, Florida, produced a booklet of nonprofit organizations in her area that seek volunteers.

Brandon Hussey of Waco, Texas, started an organization that educates peers about drugs, gangs and violence, and operates a twenty-four-hour telephone hotline to help those in trouble.

Becca Laptook of Dallas, Texas, formed a community-service group at her school that involved more than 250 classmates in volunteer projects at local hospitals, shelters, food banks, etc.

Lindsey Kulas of Windsor Locks, Connecticut, worked with a local Lions Club to form a community-service group that hosts dances, cleans elderly people's homes, and prepares food for a soup kitchen.

Ben Moore of Riverton, Utah, challenged students at his school to collectively render 1,000 hours of volunteer service over a special two-week period.

Alissa Tippetts of Blackfoot, Idaho, recruited more than fifty students to create a "summer service club" that painted a retirement home, held a car wash fund-raiser, and assisted the elderly.

Jeffrey Walker of Henderson, Nevada, developed a book for high school students on how to identify and create community-service projects and sent it to class presidents at other schools.

Annina Burns of Falls Church, Virginia, founded a youth volunteer group called "Y-NOT" that tutors homeless children six hours a week and sells calendars featuring drawings by the children to raise money for their shelter.

Amy Cada of Downers Grove, Illinois, launched a youth organization that encourages students to collect soft drink "pop tops" to benefit Ronald McDonald Houses across the country.

Kathleen Jones of Concord, New Hampshire, started an environmental group at her school that helps build and maintain hiking trails, conducts recycling programs, and plants trees.

Launch a Collection Drive for Needed Items

Katie Rudoff of Green River, Wyoming, organized a "scavenger hunt" food drive that involved several teams competing to see who could collect the most donated food.

Dev SenGupta of Renton, Washington, implemented a toy and book drive that yielded 5,000 items to benefit homeless children at shelters in his area.

Kelly Shelinsky of Philadelphia, Pennsylvania, collected new and used books and donated them to a local children's hospital.

Stephanie Adas of West Bloomfield, Michigan, persuaded classmates to donate more than 100 pair of unneeded, "gently used" shoes to a local service organization.

William Vaughan of Huntsville, Alabama, collected more than 500 pieces of clothing for the homeless by setting up collection sites, soliciting door-to-door, and requesting donations from local businesses.

Heidi Larison of Towanda, Kansas, started a campaign to purchase stuffed animals for her local police, fire, and emergency medical departments to give to children in crisis situations.

Diana Gamble of Lewiston, Montana, created a program that solicits items such as diapers, blankets, toothbrushes, and coloring books from local merchants to distribute to children in foster care.

Dawn Stockwell of Westminster, Colorado, organized a group of young people to "Trick or Treat so Others Can Eat," a canned-food drive conducted the day before Halloween for a local food bank.

Celia Merendi of Miami, Florida, conducted a book drive that provided every student at a local elementary school with a new book to take home for summertime reading.

Megan Ostrem of Portland, Oregon, set up a small room in her school to serve as the "Evergreen Clothing Closet" and began collecting donations from fellow students for local migrant workers and other needy families.

Campaign Against Smoking and Substance Abuse

Mark Jones of Marion, West Virginia, dressed up as "Cowboy Dave" and traveled to schools, day care centers, scout troops, libraries, churches, and summer camps to warn youngsters about the dangers of drugs and smoking.

Joshua Hewitt of Perry, New York, staged a simulated traffic accident at his school to graphically demonstrate to other students the horrors of drunk driving.

Lauren Benson of Benton, Arkansas, developed a "buddy-check" drug-prevention program that encourages teens to pair up and support their buddies in a promise to be drug- and alcohol-free.

Emily Fischer of West Kingston, Rhode Island, rallied her student body to support a more stringent smoking policy at her school.

Marissa Olson of Lakewood, Colorado, organized a drunk-driving-simulator program at her school that enabled students to experience how it feels to drive under the influence of intoxicants.

Derek Swierczek of Palatine, Illinois, campaigned to have all cigarette vending machines removed from his town to prevent underage smoking.

Kimberly Pettersen of Minot, North Dakota, launched a public relations campaign to promote a smoke-free environment in her community and state.

Promote Health and Safety

Sara McDonnall of Lamar, Colorado, made a lap puppet named "Bucklebear" and took it to local elementary schools to deliver presentations on the importance of using seat belts.

Rafael Corona of Van Buren, Arkansas, wrote and performed a safety skit that gave young children advice about being home alone, answering the telephone, and talking to strangers.

Jennifer Eaton of Raleigh, North Carolina, led her school's Students Against Violence Everywhere (SAVE) program, which offered gun-safety instruction at elementary schools, and sponsored a variety of anti-violence activities.

Matthew Iwamoto of Indianapolis, Indiana, created a children's bicycle-safety class using interactive games and indoor and outdoor exercises.

Cody Hill of Portland, Oregon, organized a series of toy swaps called "Guns Aren't Fun" that encouraged kids to trade in their toy guns for other, non-violent toys.

Jessica Warren of Elizabethtown, North Carolina, created a presentation on food poisoning and food-handling practices and delivered it at her school and several youth camps.

Amanda Langley of Kinder, Louisiana, organized an all-girl assembly at her school to raise awareness of breast cancer.

William Fletcher of Jackson, Georgia, conducted a community-education campaign on his county's mosquito problem and how to control it.

Cory Snyder of Bowie, Maryland, spearheaded a children's fund-raising campaign to provide the volunteer fire department in his town with a device that enables firefighters to see through smoke.

Benjamin Womick of Spartanburg, South Carolina, helped save three houses from destruction and helped many people injured in accidents as a volunteer for his town's fire department.

Theodoros Milonopoulos of Studio City, California, conducted a kids' petition campaign to ban the sale of gun bullets in Los Angeles.

Encourage Respect for Others

Andrea Hurwitz of Peabody, Massachusetts, started a campaign in her school that encouraged fellow students to wear blue ribbons to express "zero tolerance" for hate graffiti and other acts of prejudice.

Christopher Chambers of Ravenswood, West Virginia, created an authentic Indian costume and learned Native American dances to participate in a program that conveys and inspires respect for the Native American spirit.

Danielle Buechler of Centerville, South Dakota, created skits featuring singing and ventriloquism to educate others about discrimination and other social issues at schools, teacher workshops, and nursing homes.

Caitlin Connolly of Cohasset, Massachusetts, formed the Social Awareness Organization at her school, which addresses social issues such as racism, sexism, homophobia, and political injustice.

Anisa Kintz of Conway, South Carolina, organized a kids' conference at Coastal Carolina University called "Calling All Colors" to promote racial unity among young people in grades three through eight.

Be a Tutor or Mentor

Adrian Hunt of Pontiac, Michigan, started a mentoring program to help boys without appropriate adult role models grow up to be responsible men.

Warren Martin of Edwards, Mississippi, tutored elementary and high school students in English, math, science, and history after school in his own home.

Alison Zitron of New York, New York, set up a creative mentoring and tutoring program called "Kids to Kids" that helped at-risk kids with schoolwork and arts and crafts projects every Saturday.

Quinn Wilhelmi of Eugene, Oregon, recruited several classmates to help him tutor fifth-grade students in writing skills at his former elementary school, working primarily on writing their autobiographies.

Pettus Randall of Tuscaloosa, Alabama, founded a program that recruits high school students to serve as reading mentors to elementary schoolchildren.

Sara Atkinson of Kailua-Kona, Hawaii, persuaded a group of friends to help her develop a mentoring program for young children ages 9 to 14 who are at risk for violence and substance abuse.

Help Young Children Discover the Joy of Reading

Donan Eckles of Hernando, Mississippi, collected used books for kids who don't have books of their own, and volunteered to read stories at local schools to encourage children to read.

Angela Lind of Flandreau, South Dakota, started a summer reading hour for young children at a local library, featuring age-appropriate books and activities that pertained to the stories.

Laura Berman of North Kingstown, Rhode Island, made presentations to third-graders on the joys of books and libraries, giving each child a personal library card and a T-shirt reading "Your library card . . . don't leave home without it."

Philana Omorotionmwan of Baton Rouge, Louisiana, performed a series of plays for elementary schoolchildren at area libraries during her summer break.

Share Your Knowledge

Amber Birner of Warrens, Wisconsin, helped more than 100 small children overcome their fear of water and learn basic swimming skills.

Burr Settles of Lexington, Kentucky, created a science-education program for elementary students that features a series of interactive demonstrations staged like a magic show.

Jay Hunt of Lansing, Kansas, founded a program that provides one youth each year a free calf to raise and breed.

Ariel Gold of Hilo, Hawaii, started a theater program for elementary school students with behavioral problems.

Shannon Blevins of Columbus, Mississippi, created a gospel choir at his school to enable young students to develop their singing talents and share fellowship.

Kristine Schmitz of Kensington, Maryland, developed a program for at-risk girls in fourth and fifth grades that provides positive female role models and focuses on issues such as self-esteem, conflict resolution, and healthy relationships.

Mariah Martin of Ft. Collins, Colorado, developed a nine-week educational and self-esteem program for second-grade students.

Morgan Aquino Mackles of Lake Oswego, Oregon, founded a "family heritage" program that teaches first- to third-graders how to collect family information and organize it into a unique family history.

Armando Martinez of Seattle, Washington, helped fund and conduct a five-week seminar that taught seventy youths from seven states how to be community leaders and resolve conflict peacefully.

Ryan Leybas of Casa Grande, Arizona, founded a leadership camp that teaches middle-level students skills to help them succeed both in school and in life.

Camila Hoff of Dagmar, Montana, planned a series of special activity days to teach local youth hands-on skills in areas such as winter survival, safety, and exploring the great outdoors.

Megan Hedgecock of El Paso, Texas, taught English to first-graders whose first language was Spanish.

Make Life a Little Brighter for Underprivileged Kids

Anna DeMartino of Malverne, New York, conducted a fundraising campaign at her school to purchase Christmas presents for a family affected by domestic violence.

David Adamiec of Westbrook, Connecticut, prepared "Kid Packs" containing clothing, toiletries, toys, and school supplies for children who are separated from their families due to domestic violence, arrest, or drug abuse.

Aubyn Burnside of Hickory, North Carolina, collected used suitcases so that children living in foster homes would not have to use trash bags for their belongings when they moved from home to home.

David Lugo of Carolina, Puerto Rico, led a campaign to donate books and games to adolescents in Puerto Rico's penitentiaries.

Eric Perlyn of Boca Raton, Florida, worked with shoe manufacturers and local shoe stores to provide new shoes to underprivileged kids.

Dominique Womack of Washington, D.C., planned a holiday shopping trip to allow disadvantaged children to buy gifts for themselves and others.

Gillian Kilberg of McLean, Virginia, used an inheritance from her grandmother to found a summer camp that provided day trips for needy and abused children.

Melissa Gillooly of Warwick, Rhode Island, started a summer tennis-education program for inner-city youngsters.

Mark Gibbs of Huntsville, Alabama, worked with his local Optimist Club and local photo stores so that more than 100 needy children had a chance to have their pictures taken with Santa Claus free of charge.

Reach out to the Needy

Emily Tobler of Orem, Utah, prepared fifty brown-bag lunches once a month for a local homeless shelter to distribute to her community's neediest people.

Anne Newman of Monroe, Louisiana, recruited a group of students at her school to spend a day at a home for teenage runaways, where they painted, cleaned up the yard and spent time with the residents.

Tim Moore of Hemet, California, helped build homes for three low-income families through Habitat for Humanity, and **Justin Carroll** of Wynne, Arkansas, founded a chapter of Habitat for Humanity at his school.

Jonathan Hoffenberg of Phoenix, Arizona, coordinated a food service that prepared and served dinner once a week to indigent people in a local school.

Brandon Mulcunry of Farmington, Connecticut, created a vegetable garden to grow produce for a homeless shelter and soup kitchen.

Amber Coffman of Glen Burnie, Maryland, prepared bag lunches and distributed them to homeless people on the streets of Baltimore.

Elisabeth Charnley of Barrington, Rhode Island, assisted families at a homeless shelter by holding a bake sale to buy needed items, obtaining gift certificates from local restaurants, babysitting children so that their parents could go to school, and delivering food, toys, books, and clothing.

Erin Campbell of Hampden, Maine, prepared home-cooked meals for a home for homeless and troubled youth.

Jamie Liles of Henderson, Kentucky, chaired a community campaign that collected coats and eyeglasses for the needy.

Sarah Hays of Alliance, Ohio, organized an overnight camp that featured games, hiking, arts and crafts projects, and an astronomy presentation for eleven girls in foster care.

Haven Scogin of Albuquerque, New Mexico, created an outreach program for at-risk kids that included a haunted house Halloween party for 100 children.

William Shurley of Monroe, Louisiana, founded a student-run organization that pairs schools with area churches to encourage church members to sponsor elementary students who cannot afford their school fees.

Vanessa Milsom of San Juan, Puerto Rico, spearheaded the construction of a home for an organization that takes care of neglected and abused boys.

Fix up Your Town or Neighborhood

Marcy Bluvas of Omaha, Nebraska, enlisted the help of twelve local children and their families to plant more than 4,000 flowers over an eight-block area.

Nathan Ladd of Effingham, Kansas, sought and obtained permission from his city clerk to restore a neglected flower garden in a city park.

Madeleine Elish of Pittsburgh, Pennsylvania, and seventeen friends painted over graffiti at four city locations.

Andrew Ingold of Andover, Kansas, conducted a penny drive to help clean up a historic home that had been vandalized by students from his school.

Emily Mathes of Vicksburg, Mississippi, lobbied local government to restore an abandoned and neglected neighborhood park that had become a hangout for drug dealers.

Robert Sheerer of Cedar Falls, Iowa, designed and constructed a self-guided nature trail in a local park, and **Jason Hall** of Salisbury,

North Carolina, built a twenty-four-foot pedestrian bridge for a park in his community.

Charles Darus of Cairo, Georgia, organized a group of young people to help renovate a building for a youth center in his town and to help fund its operating costs.

Alan Simpson of Fort Atkinson, Wisconsin, started a fund-raising campaign to save and restore an old fort in his community.

Eddie Armstrong of North Little Rock, Arkansas, helped rebuild a dilapidated and dangerous playground in his apartment complex.

Jacob Schanzenbach of Rosalia, Washington, designed and implemented a new address system for his town to make it easier for emergency services to locate homes quickly.

Kimberly Sanchez of Rio Piedras, Puerto Rico, raised money and recruited volunteers to restore a children's ward at a local hospital.

Charles Andrews of Bradenton, Florida, organized a project to stop soil erosion on an ancient and historically significant Indian mound near his home.

Scott Stevens of Saratoga, Wyoming, mobilized his town to renovate his town's athletic track.

Jennifer Larson of Spearfish, South Dakota, organized a backyard carnival to raise money for a new library.

Monica Brady of Philadelphia, Pennsylvania, formed an "environmental society" at her school that sought to restore a sense of pride and community to her inner-city neighborhood by cleaning up graffiti and planting trees and flowers.

Trent Anderson of Benjamin, Utah, constructed a tribute to his town's history on a small plot of land, with informational plaques, a bench, and a fence.

Be True to Your School

John Bollhardt of Shaftsbury, Vermont, coordinated a drive to collect used clothing, sold the clothes to a recycling company, and used the proceeds to buy textbooks for his school.

Jesse Waite of Logandale, Nevada, designed a landscaping project to beautify an empty lot at a local elementary school.

Aaron Soto of Las Cruces, New Mexico, prepared and conducted a four-day instructional seminar that taught teachers at his school how to use computers.

Jennifer Nydegger of Townsend, Montana, canvassed local businesses, clubs, and organizations to raise money to provide a flagpole for her school.

Katherine Lindle of Louisville, Kentucky, converted an unused room at her Catholic school into a chapel to provide a place of peace and solitude for fellow students.

Amanda Chapman of Staten Island, New York, provided a volunteer baby-sitting service during school PTA meetings.

Marc Freed-Finnegan of Montclair, New Jersey, started an on-line bulletin board to help classmates keep track of homework assignments.

Kyle Loberg of Missoula, Montana, built picnic tables for his school after acquiring donated lumber, drafting a design, and recruiting members of his Boy Scout troop.

Christopher Haagen of Moscow, Idaho, built a professional lighting and sound-control booth for his high school auditorium.

James French of Goshen, Kentucky, organized a student-run fundraising organization that raised more than $2,000 to fund athletics, fine arts, media, technology and co-curricular activities for his school.

Protect the Environment

Dillon Denisen of Grand Meadow, Minnesota, created and delivered presentations on the importance and techniques of recycling.

Kathleen Jones of Concord, New Hampshire, launched an environmental group at her school that helps build and maintain hiking trails, conducts recycling programs, and plants trees throughout her county.

Jenny Reed of Hixson, Tennessee, formed a "Green Team" within her 4-H club that cleaned up state parks, planted food plots for wild animals, taught inner-city youth about the environment, and planned hands-on activities to foster conservation.

Jason Harper of Grand Island, Nebraska, promoted groundwater protection through speeches, presentations, puppet shows, public-service announcements, a newsletter, and guided tours.

Robbie Hanson of Cave Junction, Oregon, worked with a local sanitation facility to found a recycling club at his school that processes close to thirty tons of paper per month.

Amber Novotny of Rosholt, South Dakota, established a recycling center for newspapers, magazines, plastic, tin, and glass in her small town.

Heather Hitzman of Florence, Oregon, led her seventh-grade class in a project to test and clean up a Coho salmon stream.

Aaron Dickson of Clovis, New Mexico, organized a community-wide "trash bash" that rallied volunteers to clean up 155 city blocks.

Juan Ramirez of San Juan, Puerto Rico, took scuba-diving lessons and then joined efforts to clean up the ocean floor.

Zachary Adkison of Cheyenne, Wyoming, and his classmates spent three days removing garbage from Crow Creek, clearing overgrowth and planting flowers and bushes.

Take Care of Animals

Rachel Salzer of Rootstown, Ohio, volunteered for the local Animal Protective League, taking care of abandoned or mistreated pets, and holding a candy sale to raise money for the league.

Aaron Crim of West Valley City, Utah, collected blankets for newborn and sick animals in the Salt Lake City Zoo's hospital.

Sabrina Lojuk of Carrollton, Texas, helped take care of animals at a local animal shelter, helped with adoptions, and gave speeches on animal-related issues.

Megan Wardwell of Boise, Idaho, worked at her local Humane Society chapter, feeding and walking animals and cleaning their cages.

Work with Senior Citizens

Lauren Garsten of Cheshire, Connecticut, set up a program that matches up senior citizens, abused children, and high school student volunteers in groups of three and organizes outings for them.

Erin Eno of Kahului, Hawaii, sewed lap blankets and wheelchair bags for nursing home residents.

Benjamin Fiske of Washington, D.C., volunteered at a home for the elderly, transporting residents, preparing food, answering telephones, helping nurses, and providing companionship.

Jill Feyereisen of Gregory, South Dakota, created personalized birthday and "get well" cards for nursing home residents.

Mindi Kimp of Corvallis, Montana, organized a formal dance "prom" for local senior citizens the night before her own high school prom.

Kristyn Nordfors of Brewer, Maine, read stories and poems to residents of a nursing home, and organized an arts-and-crafts night.

Michelle Turbin of Wisconsin Rapids, Wisconsin, created a program called "The Night Before Christmas" that brings children into local nursing homes on Christmas Eve to spread the joy of the holiday.

Jenna Brown of Louisville, Kentucky, helped with games and activities at a local nursing home, delivered mail to residents, and helped with bookkeeping and clerical duties.

Gabrielle Willis of Anchorage, Alaska, volunteered as an editor, reporter, photographer, and graphic designer for a newspaper at an assisted-living/nursing facility in her town.

Kelly Linquist of Fonda, Iowa, made weekly visits to a nursing home, playing cards and bingo with the residents, entertaining them with her pet dog and kittens, and raising money to buy them holiday gifts.

Sarah Bonady of Wynne, Arkansas, persuaded her 4-H club to adopt a retirement center, where club members coordinate fashion shows, holiday visits, craft activities, and outdoor planting projects.

Tricia Geyer of Milford, Delaware, organized a Christmas Dinner Theater for senior citizens and sold tables to local businesses to pay for a turkey dinner, a play, music and dancing.

Provide Comfort or Support to Those in Crisis

Jon Wagner-Holtz of Mission Viejo, California, formed a group that provides friendship, education, understanding, and support for kids who have a parent with cancer.

Sharifa Ramaileh of Bountiful, Utah, created plaster hand and foot molds of terminally ill children as keepsakes for family members in association with a children's hospice agency.

Ruth King of Princeton, West Virginia, served at a local crisis pregnancy center as a peer counselor to young women experiencing unexpected pregnancies.

Brittany Blockman of Memphis, Tennessee, founded a support group for teens and young adults who have a parent or close family member with cancer.

Brenda Corace of Palm Harbor, Florida, started a video project that provides families of terminally ill patients with a "living" record of their loved ones after they're gone.

Molly Farneth of Wilmington, Delaware, recruited fellow students to prepare meals for families of sick children who are staying at a local Ronald McDonald House.

Ashleigh Rowsam of Oklahoma City, Oklahoma, assisted teen mothers with basic needs like food and clothing at an Infant Crisis Center.

Leslie Coggins of Phenix City, Alabama, made burial gowns for premature infants who cannot survive, as a way of easing their families' pain.

Pitch in When Disaster Strikes

Craig Whyte of Blackfoot, Idaho, organized a "day-away" camp for children left homeless by a massive flood.

Sofia Blazevic of Guaynabo, Puerto Rico, distributed medical supplies and clothing to victims of Hurricane Hortense.

Zachary Carter of Arlington, Virginia, and his classmates sold small, paper teddy bears to raise $1,500 for children affected by the Oklahoma City bombing.

Sara Stieben of Fort Collins, Colorado, helped people in her town pump water from their homes, salvage their belongings, and deliver food and clothing donations after a major flood.

Geneva Campbell of Philomath, Oregon, and fellow students baked and sold thousands of cookies to help relief efforts in Oklahoma City after the bombing of a federal office building there.

Think and Act Globally

Kiara Diggs of Washington, D.C., spent a month in Mexico with the Amigos de las Americas helping residents of a poor village design and construct latrines and learn sanitation procedures.

Sarra Cherry of Albuquerque, New Mexico, solicited donations of eyeglasses and sent them to a tribe in Indonesia.

Tabitha Kulish of Lancaster, Pennsylvania, made homemade greeting cards for U.S. military personnel overseas and others in need of cheering up.

Elizabeth Shenk of Westerville, Ohio, raised money and volunteered for Operation Smile, an organization that performs free reconstructive surgery on deformed children in Third World countries.

Dianna English of Willimantic, Connecticut, founded the Connecticut chapter of Free the Children, a non-profit youth organization dedicated to eliminating child labor and exploitation around the world.

Or Do Something Else

Justin Eveloff of Council Bluffs, Iowa, persuaded his state to declare a special day in recognition of the needs and importance of children, then organized a community youth celebration on that day.

Jason Kelley of Prescott, Arizona, created a youth chamber of commerce in his town to "provide kids who are leaders and entrepreneurs with an outlet for business opportunities."

Robert Purvis of Tucson, Arizona, volunteered as a teen lawyer representing first-time juvenile misdemeanor offenders during sentencing trials in Tucson's Teen Court program.

Adrien Lopez of Valdez, Alaska, established a forum called Teens Against Pregnancy to educate young girls about the challenges of being a teen mother.

Tyler Mann of Roswell, Georgia, and **Christine Varnado** of Hattiesburg, Mississippi, conducted voter registration drives at their schools.

Randi Pope of Long Beach, Mississippi, founded a group at her school to fight negative peer pressure, partly by recognizing on the school's morning news show students who perform special acts of kindness.

April Matthews of Woodbridge, Virginia, started a support group for kids at a homeless center, comprised of young people who had previously been homeless themselves.

Jason Cunningham of Dallas, Texas, initiated a statewide program to raise money for the restoration of a historic battleship.

Appendix C

Organizations and Internet Sites

Following is a sampling of organizations and Internet sites where you can learn more about volunteering.

Action Without Borders
www.idealist.org

A searchable list of 20,000 organizations that use volunteers, as well as other community service resources; add your own.

Activism 2000 Project
P.O. Box E
Kensington, Maryland 20895
(800) KID–POWER

e-mail: info@youthactivism.com
www.youthactivism.com

A clearinghouse and network to encourage maximum youth participation in democracy and community service.

American Red Cross
Program and Services Department
Youth Associate
431 18th Street, NW
Washington, DC 20006

e-mail: info@usa.redcross.org
www.redcross.org/youth/

Contribute to a variety of Red Cross services in your own community.

American Youth Foundation
1315 Ann Avenue
St. Louis, MO 63104

e-mail: mail@ayf.com
www.ayf.com

Leadership and community service activities.

America's Charities
12701 Fair Lakes Circle,
Suite 370
Fairfax, VA 22033
(800) 458-9505

e-mail: info@charities.org
www.charities.org

Network of charities nationwide.

America's Promise
909 N. Washington Street, Suite 400
Alexandria, VA 22314
www.americaspromise.org

America's Promise/Alliance for Youth, led by General Colin Powell, is dedicated to ensuring that young people have access to resources needed to become successful adults.

AOL Foundation
www.helping.org

Search by zip code for volunteer opportunities close to home.

Boy Scouts of America
1325 West Walnut Hill Lane
Irving, TX 75015-2079

www.bsa.scouting.org

Teaching positive values and leadership skills to youth.

Boys and Girls Clubs of America
1230 West Peachtree Street, NW
Atlanta, GA 30309-3447

e-mail: KLodhi@bgca.org
www.bgca.org

Teens can participate in community service in clubs for leadership development.

Campus Outreach Opportunity League (COOL)
1531 P Street, NW, Suite LL
Washington, DC 20005

e-mail: homeoffice@cool2serve.org
www.cool2serve.org

Network and database of programs for college-age and other youth volunteers.

Child Welfare League of America
440 First Street, NW, Third Floor
Washington, DC 20001-2085

www.cwla.org

An association of agencies helping children.

City Year
285 Columbus Avenue
Boston, MA 02116

www.city-year.org

An organization whose goals include inspiring youth ages 17 to 24 to perform a year of full-time community service. Short-term volunteer opportunities also.

Corporation for National Service
1201 New York Avenue, NW
Washington, DC 20525

e-mail: webmaster@cns.gov
www.cns.gov

Matches people with opportunities to serve.

Do Something
423 West 55th Street, 8th Floor
New York, NY 10019

e-mail: mail@dosomething.org
www.dosomething.org

Helps youth get involved in service in their communities.

Earth Force
1908 Mt. Vernon Avenue,
Second Floor
Alexandria, VA 22301

e-mail: earthforce@earthforce.org
www.earthforce.org

Youth solving environmental problems in their communities.

Excel Clubs
National Exchange Club
3050 Central Ave.
Toledo, OH 43606-1700
(800) 924-2643

*e-mail:*nechq@aol.com
www.nationalexchangeclub.com/.htm

Service clubs for high school youth.

Future Problem Solving Program
Community Problem Solving
2500 Packard Road, Suite 110
Ann Arbor, MI 48104-6827
(800) 256-1499

www.fpsp.org

Applying creative thinking to real community problems.

Girl Scouts of the U.S.A.
420 Fifth Avenue
New York, NY 10018-2702
*e-mail:*misc@gsa.org
www.gsusa.org

An organization for girls to learn leadership and help the community.

Girls Incorporated
120 Wall Street, Third Floor
New York, NY 10005

*e-mail:*girlsincorporated@girlsinc.org
www.girlsinc.org

Programs for girls 6 to 18 at 1,000 sites nationwide.

Habitat for Humanity International
121 Habitat Street
Americus, GA 31709

e-mail: public_info@habitat.org
www.habitat.org

Ways for kids ages 5 and up to help provide housing for the needy.

IMPACT Online
www.impactonline.org

Free online matching service for volunteers and nonprofit organizations.

Independent Sector
1200 18th Street, NW
Washington, DC 20036

e-mail: info@independentsector.org
www.indepsec.org

Search for volunteer opportunties.

Internet Nonprofit Center
www.nonprofits.org

Information about nonprofits and volunteering.

Key Club International
3636 Woodview Trace
Indianapolis, IN 46268

e-mail: Kiwanismail@kiwanis.org

www.kiwanis.org

Offers Builders Clubs for service-minded middle schoolers, Key Clubs for high schoolers.

Kidlink
www.kidlink.org

A global e-mail network of kids around the world. Volunteers needed to help things run smoothly.

Kids Care Clubs
P.O. Box 1083
New Canaan, CT 06840

e-mail: kids.care@kidscare.org
www.kidscare.org

Clubs and projects for all ages.

Kids F.A.C.E.
(Kids for a Clean Environment)
P.O. Box 158254
Nashville, TN 37215

e-mail: kidsface@mindspring.com
www.kidsface.org

An international children's environmental organization with 300,000 members worldwide.

National 4-H Council
7100 Connecticut Avenue
Chevy Chase, MD 20815

www.fourhcouncil.edu

A youth organization with numerous programs for learning and community service.

National Service Resource Center
ETR Associates
P.O. Box 1830
Santa Cruz, CA 95061-1830
(800) 860-2684

e-mail: nsrc@etr.org
www.etr-associates.org/NSRC/

This site provides information and resources for service organizations.

National Youth Leadership Council
1910 West County Road B
St. Paul, MN 55113
e-mail: nylcinfo@nylc.org
www.nylc.org
Advocacy and training for service learning programs.

Points of Light Foundation
1400 I Street, NW, Suite 800
Washington, DC 20005
e-mail: volnet@pointsoflight.org
www.pointsoflight.org
Mobilizing people and resources to deliver creative solutions to community problems; includes contact info for family volunteering.

The Prudential Spirit of Community Initiative
The Prudential Insurance
Company of America
751 Broad St.
Newark, NJ 07102-3777
e-mail: spirit@prudential.com
www.prudential.com/community
A series of programs, including awards, to inspire young people to improve their communities by volunteering.

Save the Children
54 Wilton Road
Westport, CT 06880
(800) 243-5075
www.savethechildren.org
Opportunities for your school or organization to help children in crisis around the world by raising much-needed funds.

Stand for Children
1834 Connecticut Ave. NW
Washington, DC 20009
(800) 663-4032
e-mail: tellstand@stand.org
www.stand.org
A nationwide grassroots movement; join or start a Stand for Children chapter in your community to help ensure that all children can grow up healthy, educated, and safe.

Teens, Crime, and the Community
c/o Street Law, Inc.
1600 K Street, NW, Suite 602
Washington, DC 20006
e-mail: tcc@ncpc.org
www.nationaltcc.org
A national program for teens to get involved in crime prevention; free newsletter.

Voices of Youth
*e-mail:*voy@unicef.org
www.unicef.org/voy/
The Voices of Youth program involves problem-solving discussions among children around the world. Take quizzes and visit "The Meeting Place" to discuss how you can take action and express your opinion on vital issues such as children's rights and children in war.

Volunteers of America, Inc.
110 S. Union Street
Alexandria, VA 22314
(800) 899-0089
e-mail: voa@voa.org
www.voa.org
Numerous local ways to volunteer in your community as part of this national organization.

YMCA of the USA
101 North Wacker Drive
Chicago, IL 60606
www.ymca.net

Check out the "Get Involved" section of the site for ways to volunteer at your local YMCA.

Youth as Resources

Center for Youth as Resources
1700 K Street, NW, Ste. 801
Washington, DC 20006
e-mail: yar@ncpc.org
www.yar.org
Provides small grants to young people to design and carry out service projects.

Youth Crime Watch of America

9300 South Dadeland Blvd., Ste.100
Miami, FL 33156
e-mail: ycwa@ycwa.org
www.ycwa.org
Start a group with an adult advisor, get training, help promote crime-prevention activities in your community; participate in the YCWA online club.

Youthlink

e-mail: peter@youthlink.org
www.youthlink.org
Download a "Youth Action Guide" to start your own youth service group, find out what others are doing to make a difference.

Youth Service America

1101 15th Street, NW, Suite 200
Washington, DC 20005
www.servenet.org/ysa/
A resource center to help young people find ways to volunteer and serve their communities, including project ideas and information about Youth Service Day. Click on ServeNet to be matched with volunteer opportunities according to your zip code.

Youth Venture

www.youthventure.org
A variety of community-spirited projects are listed under Ventures and Resources.

Youth Volunteer Corps of America

4600 W. 51st Street, Suite 300
Overland Park, KS 66205
e-mail: yvca@yvca.org
www.yvca.org
Volunteer opportunities for ages 11 to 18; click on Youth Opportunities. Many useful links.

Youth Work Links and Ideas

www.youthwork.com
This site has a large collection of links to other related sites.

Appendix D

Projects of the Teens in This Book

The following award-winning volunteer projects are continuing in one form or another and welcome your involvement:

Gabriella Contreras: For a packet of information on how to start your own Club B.A.D.D.D., including a full-color booklet and a video, send $33.20 *(includes postage)* to: Club B.A.D.D.D., P.O. Box 85256, Tucson, AZ 85754.

Kristen Deaton: For a free how-to packet about "Anyone Can Softball," *e-mail* Kristen: *kristentu@aol.com* or write her c/o Scott Peterson, Prudential Insurance Company of America, 751 Broad Street, 16th floor, Newark, NJ 07102.

Lo Detrich: The Cystic Fibrosis Foundation can be contacted by mail: 6931 Arlington Rd., Bethesda, MD 20814; by phone: (800) FIGHT CF (344-4823); by e-mail: *info@cff.org.* The Great Strides page of the CFF Internet site is *www.cff.org/GREATSTRIDES.htm.* See Appendix E for information about *The Spirit of Lo,* a book written by Lo's parents *(www.SpiritofLo.com)*

Emily Douglas: Grandma's Gifts, P.O. Box 340452, Columbus, OH 43235; e-mail *GrndmaGfts@aol.com; http://hometown.aol.com/grandmagfts*

David Levitt: For information about USA Harvest, call 1-800-USA-4FOOD. For information about Tampa Bay Harvest, check *www.tampabayharvest.org.* To reach David about Operation Food for Thought, e-mail him at *celebrate9@aol.com.*

Jamie Morales: To request a program by Jamie, or for more information, contact Sandy Hysom by e-mail: *shysom@feist.com*

Tyrell Nickens: To help "Ty's Friends," contact Tyrell c/o Scott Peterson, Prudential Insurance Company of America, 751 Broad Street, 16th floor, Newark, NJ 07102.

Alisia Orosco: Project Hugs, P.O. Box 225, 4102 Buffalo Gap Rd., Ste. F, Abilene, TX 79605-7234.

For more information on The Prudential Spirit of Community Awards: write to Scott Peterson, Prudential Insurance Company of America, 751 Broad Street, 16th floor,Newark, NJ 07102. You can also send e-mail to *spirit@prudential.com* or visit the company on the Web at *www.prudential.com/community.*

Appendix E

Books for Further Information

The following books contain stories about young volunteers and a great deal of useful information about how you can find and participate in a successful project.

Adams, Patricia, Jean Marzollo, and Jeff Moores. *The Helping Hands Handbook: A Guidebook for Kids Who Want to Help People, Animals, and the World We Live In.* New York: Random House, 1992.

DeLisle, Jim. *Kid Stories: Biographies of 20 Young People You'd Like to Know.* Minneapolis: Free Spirit Publishing, 1991.

Detrich, Terry and Don. *The Spirit of Lo: An Ordinary Family's Extraordinary Journey.* Tulsa: Mind Matters, Inc., 2000.

Duper, Linda Leeb. *160 Ways to Help the World: Community Service Projects for Young People.* New York: Facts on File, 1996.

Erickson, Judith B. *Directory of American Youth Organizations: A Guide to 500 Clubs, Groups, Troops, Teams, Societies, Lodges, and More for Young People,* seventh edition. Minneapolis: Free Spirit Publishing, 1998.

Erlbach, Arlene. *The Kids' Volunteering Book.* Minneapolis: Lerner Publications, 1998.

Goodman, Alan. *The Big Help Book: 365 Ways You Can Make a Difference.* New York: Pocket Books, 1994.

Hollander, Jeffrey, and Linda Catling. *How to Make the World a Better Place: 116 Ways You Can Make a Difference.* New York: Norton, 1995.

Hoose, Phillip. *It's Our World, Too!: Stories of Young People Who Are Making a Difference.* Boston: Little, Brown and Company, 1993.

Karnes, Frances A., and Suzanne M. Bean. *Girls and Young Women Leading the Way: 20 True Stories About Leadership.* Minneapolis: Free Spirit Publishing, 1993.

Lesko, Wendy Schaetzel, and Emanuel Tsourounis II. *Youth! The 26% Solution.* Kensignton, MD: Activism 2000 Project, 1998.

Lewis, Barbara A. *The Kid's Guide to Service Projects: Over 500 Service Ideas for Young People Who Want to Make a Difference.* Minneapolis: Free Spirit Publishing, 1995.

——. *The Kid's Guide to Social Action,* revised edition. Minneapolis: Free Spirit Publishing, 1998.

——. *Kids with Courage: True Stories about Young People Making a Difference.* Minneapolis: Free Spirit Publishing, 1992.

Westridge Young Writers Workshop. *Kids Explore: Kids Who Make a Difference.* Santa Fe: John Muir, 1997.

About the Author

Susan K. Perry, Ph.D., is a social psychologist, an award-winning article writer, and an author of nonfiction books. Her book, *Writing in Flow: Keys to Enhanced Creativity,* was a best-seller. She also wrote the award-winning *Playing Smart* and *Fun Time, Family Time,* among others. Perry has written more than 700 articles on topics ranging from family to relationships to psychology for publications such as *Seventeen, Teen, USA Today,* the *Los Angeles Times, Child, Parenting, Billboard,* and others. She is a longtime contributing editor for the regional publications *Valley* and *L.A. Parent,* for which she has written a nationally syndicated column on parenting books.

Perry won the Outstanding Service Article Award from the American Society of Journalists and Authors, and the First Place Award of Excellence for Feature Writing given by the Parenting Publications of America. She has frequently been featured as a psychology expert on TV, radio, and in magazines.

Perry has taught writing through the extension departments of the University of California Los Angeles, University of California Irvine, California State University Fullerton, Santa Monica College, and Glendale Community College. She also teaches online courses for Writer's Digest and is a writing consultant. In addition, she is an adjunct instructor of psychology at Woodbury University in Burbank, California. She has two grown sons and lives in Los Angeles with her husband, the poet Stephen Perry. Her Internet home is http://www.bunnyape.com.

Notes